MR. KNIFE, MISS FORK

MR. KNIFE
MISS FORK

Number 1

CONTENTS

Introduction 5
Alexei Kruchenykh [Russia] Two Poems 9
Amelia Rosselli [Italy] from *War Variations* 19
José Antonio Mazzotti [Peru] Two Poems 25
Eduardo Chironos [Peru] Pirate of Memory 31
Ishihara Yoshirô [Japan] Three Poems 36
Benjamin Péret [France] The Four Elements 40
Marcelin Pleynet [France] *Dogana* 48
Pablo Picasso [Spain] The Dream and Lie of General Franco 61
Miroslav Holub [Czech Republic] A Not-So-Brief Reflection on an
        Edict 62
Ştefan Agustin Doinaş [Romania] Two Poems 71
Gilbert Sorrentino [USA] A Connoisseur's Guide to the Bay Area 76
Andrea Zanzotto [Italy] (THAT) (IT GROW) 87
Friederike Mayröcker [Austria] Three Poems 93
Elisabeth Borchers [Germany] Three Poems 103
Durs Grünbein [Germany] Two Poems 113
Ronald Johnson [USA] Naps & Purrs of My Cat, Tom 122
Pentii Saarikoski [Finland] from *Trilogy* 130

COMMENTARY

Jacques Roubaud [France] About 137
Vicente Huidobro [Chile] Manifesto Mayhaps 141
Takahashi Mutsuo [Japan] The Poem of 1999 147
Will Alexander [USA] The Caribbean: Language as Translucent
        Imminence 154

REVIEWS

AMERICAN POETRY

Jeff Clark *The Little Door Slides Back* [note]   160

Fanny Howe *One Crossed Out* (Diane Ward)   160

Ann Lauterbach *On a Stair* (Martha Ronk)   161

Tom Mandel *Ancestral Cave* (Douglas Messerli)   162

Fiona Templeton *Cells of Release* (Steve Dickison)   162

Keith Waldrop *The Silhouette of the Bridge* (Douglas Messerli)   164

Barrett Watten *Frame (1971–1990)* [note]   165

BRITISH POETRY

David Miller *Collected Poems* (Dennis Phillips)   165

POETRY IN FRENCH

Oscarine Bosquet *Cromo* (Guy Bennett)   167

Alain Veinstein *Even a Child* (Douglas Messerli)   168

POETRY IN ITALIAN

Luigi Ballerini *The Cadence of the Neighboring Tribe* [note]   168

Elio Pagliarani *La pieta oggetiva (Poesie 1947–1997)* (Paul Vangelisti)   169

Andrea Zanzotto *Peasants Wake for Fellini's Casanova* (Paul Vangelisti)   171

POETRY IN JAPANESE

Violet Kazue de Cristoforo *May Sky* [note]   172

Hayashi Fumiko *I Saw a Pale Horse* and *Selected Poems from Diary of a Vababond* (Douglas Messerli)   173

Takahashi Mutsuo *Voice Garden: Selected Poems* (Douglas Messerli)   175

POETRY IN NORWEGIAN

Paal-Helge Haugen *Wintering with the Light* [note]   176

POETRY IN PORTUGUESE

Eugénio de Andrade *Another Name for Earth / O outro Nome da Terra* (Douglas Messerli)   176

Michael Palmer, Régis Bonvicino and Nelson Ascher, eds. *Nothing the Sun Could Not Explain: 20 Contemporary Brazilian Poets* [note]   177

POETRY IN SPANISH

Ernesto Livon Grosman, ed. *The XUL Reader* (Douglas Messerli)   178

POETRY IN TURKISH

Ece Ayhan *A Blind Cat Black* and *Orthodoxies* [note]   179

Mr. Knife, Miss Fork

AN ANTHOLOGY OF INTERNATIONAL POETRY

Douglas Messerli, ed.

©1998 by Sun & Moon Press / all rights reserved

Sun & Moon Press · 6026 Wilshire Boulevard, Los Angeles, California 90036

Mr. Knife, Miss Fork

As we approach the end of this century, I cannot say that I see the end of mankind, as does Takahashi Mutsuo in his fascinating essay published in this issue. But one doesn't have to be a great seer to perceive that our various cultures, and, in particular the roles of language in our societies, are in for some very difficult times in the 2000th year since the Christian religion decided that it should define itself as the beginning of a new time. In economics, in communication, and in travel we speak increasingly of a globalization of culture, which many, in turn, see as a positive force in our society—the presumption being, evidently, that as we are brought together under one intertwined economy and interconnected system of information, differences and fears will disappear. We will be "united" at least in our financial affairs and in our knowlege of the world and its events. And presumably, this interdependence will help us (if not *force* us) to work together since we all share interrelated "interests."

There is no question that such a "globalization" is taking place; but whether it will produce the rainbow of good-thinking some imagine is another matter. One might even question whether such interdependence is a good thing, particularly after witnessing the recent collapses of the economies of several Asian countries brought on, in part, by Western investments. I'll leave those questions to the economists.

However, we must question the role of language in all of this. In this scenario of global bundling (the practice of unmarried couples of early New England in which they "safely" cohabited the same bed), what is the future of language, that through which we make meaning and define ourselves? Must we envision a sort of *Blade Runner*-like argot in which the essences of various languages (rather like the essences of different herbs and vegetables in a big stewpot) are blended to give us something yet more abstract? I'm all for "bundling" or even for all out intercourse, but not if it means losing difference and its attendant complexity, for that's what excites me in all aspects of life. How disappointed I was on a recent trip to

Oslo, for example—a city which thrilled me at age 16 when I lived in Norway—to witness how American this small city had become. It was a bit like a trip to an American shopping mall, those bland centers of commerce, with virtually the same stores (with small variations) in city after city throughout the U.S. Obviously, many tourists enjoy this homogenity. But language, unlike shopping malls, is destroyed by homogenization. The more we lose the subtleties and nuances of words, the more words we abandon, the less possibility we have to express ourselves or to understand ourselves in a future that gives even optimists alarm.

Poetry delights in the complex. It is how words *might* mean, *could* mean, or *should* mean, as well as what they *do* mean that is the subject of poetry. As surely as economists study market trends, agricultural resources, various currencies, and the intelligence and stamina of industrial leaders, so must poets explore how and why people make meaning, as well as what meaning *is* itself. Philosophy, politics, history, and a knowledge of all the arts are essential tools in this exploration. But while a winnowing down of many economies into a few might make things easier for the economist, a collapsing of many languages into a few would take away the tools of the poet and, ultimately, destroy his or her reason for existing. The poet's job is to explore possibilities of meaning, which is to say possibilities of thought. Perhaps my own aversion to narrative poetry, for example, is not because I am uninterested in narrative—I am a fiction writer as well as a poet—but because poetry does not so much explore where we have *been* (the "history" of language and people that is at the heart of narrative) but where we are *going*, where we might possibly *arrive*.

It reminds me a bit of those computers in the Pentagon playing out all the possibilities of warfare: what if this happened? and we responded this way? or another way? and they responded this or that way? etc. One of the major roles of the poet is to explore all the possibilities of expression: what if this word were to be placed beside that one? what if that other word were to be linked to this? what if a word meant ten things to five different parts of the sentence? what if when we said *this* we truly meant *that*? etc.

Let us hope that the result of the poets' efforts will be more felicitous than that of the war-makers—although they would argue that in these games they are attempting to prevent war not create it. But here, of course, the metaphor must end; for the poet *is* a creator, a creator of complexity, of possibility itself. If the culture pays no attention, does not heed the possibilities of language, it can never hope to understand what or why the future might mean, or even *how* to mean in the future's grip.

It is in this context—in my understanding of the role of the poet as a seeker of complexity and difference—that I begin this journal. One might say that the simple utensils, knife and fork, which—if we are among the tribes that eat cooked food—we all use, are like those of language, something we all use that helps us to survive. Surely the child of René Crevel's novel *Babylon*, from which I've borrowed these figures, did not see the knife and the fork as simple things; for her they represented as well her cousin Cynthia and the father with whom the cousin had run off, they were the "Beautiful English woman" and her papa dressed in white flannel trousers sailing across the tablecloth of the Atlantic Ocean. With a little imaginative editing, I hope through this journal to sail the seven seas, bringing together within its pages the writing of poets from all languages and cultures of the twentieth century, celebrating their differences, their seeming impenetrabilities as opposed to the frozen Esperanto of sameness.

And so too will our similarities be revealed. So too will our humanities be shared.

This first issue is, in part, a model of what I hope to continue: poetry, in new translations and bi-lingually presented, from both contemporary, younger writers and older or more established poets, living and dead; commentary by three or four poets; and short reviews of new translations of poetry and books of poetry as they appear in their original language. To accomplish these ambitious goals, of course, I will need the participation of many poetic communities throughout the world, including academics, independent translators, and authors. Working toward this, I have put together an advisory board—which serves also in this role to the larger Sun & Moon Project for Innovative Poetry—which will ultimately support new translations of international poetry in Sun & Moon's Classics series and by other presses. But I seek and need the help of all readers. As in this issue, I will continue to involve myself in all aspects of editing, reviewing, and occasional commentary. But this activity is meaningful only if I am joined by all who care about poetry. I am willing to play the knife (my name in Swiss-German means "little knife," the eating utensil), but only with the dance of the fork can we celebrate the feast.

I have already been blessed with many of the ingredients necessary for such a feast with a supportive, loyal, and extraordinarily talented staff of Diana Daves (our eagle-eyed managing editor), Guy Bennett (a brilliant typographer who brings the knowledge of three languages, French, Italian and Russian), and the gifted interns Thérèse Bachand, Angela Kang, and Alexandra Mattraw. In a city that already reflects the global experience of our future, I am fortunate to have a wonderful group of friends who offer the resources of several languages and an intense love of writing. For the current issue Sanda Agalidi, Will Alexander, Gilbert Alter-Gilbert, Michael Henry Heim, Dennis Phillips, Martha Ronk, Julian Semilian, Paul Vangelisti and Diane Ward all contributed significantly and made themselves available for advice, translating and reviewing, and, along with Steve Dickison, Serge Gavronsky, Jack Hirschman, Anselm Hollo, Peggy Miller, Lucia Re, G. J. Racz, Jerome Rothenberg, Hiroaki Sato, Andrew Shields, and Rosmarie Waldrop, made this issue possible. My love and appreciation to them all. Finally, I thank our board of advisors, some of whose work appears in this issue; I am certain that no magazine has been offered the services of a more prestigious and knowledgeable gathering of poets.

—DOUGLAS MESSERLI

Alexei Kruchenykh

Two Poems

Translated from the Russian by Jack Hirschman
Alexander Kohav and Benjamin Zeitlin

ЗИМА

Мизиз...
    Зынь...
        Ицив.—
    Зима!...
Замороженные
Стень
Стынь...
Снегота... Снегота!...
Стужа... вьюжа...
Вью—ю—ю—га   сту—у—у—га...
Стугота... стугота!...
Убийство без крови...
Тифозное небо—одна сплошная вошь!...
Но вот
С окосевших небес
Выпало колесо
Всех растрясло
Лихорадкой и громом
И к жизни воззвало
ХАРКНУВ В ТУНДРЫ
    ПРОНЗИТЕЛЬНОЙ
        КРОВЬЮ
            ЦВЕТОВ...
—У—а!... родился ЦАП в дахе
Снежки—пах!—пах!
В зубах ззудки...
Роет яму в парном снегу—
У—гу—гу—гу!... Каракурт!... Гы—гы—гы!...
Бура—а—ан... Гора ползет—
    Зу—зу—зу—зу...
Горим... горим—го—го—го...
В недрах дикий гудрон гудит—
    ГУ—ГУ—ГУР...

Fzorz…
   Zunn…
      Itseeen…
   Winter!
The frozen
Shaddowwalla
Coolall…
Snowness…snowness!
Frostover…stormover…
Snow-w-ws-torm   fror-m-m…
Frostness…frostness!
It's bloodless murder…
The typhoid sky's a total lirefield!
But now
A wheel's dropped out
Of the obliqued heavens
Everyone's jolted
By ague and thunder
Appealing to life:
REGURGITATING INTO TUNDRAS
   WITH THE SHRILL
      BLOOD OF
         FLOWERS…
—Ooh-ah! An EGRE's born on the roof
Snowballs splaat! splaat!
Ttthooter's in the teeth…
He's digging a pit in the steamy snow—
Ooo-hoo-hoo-hoo! A karakurt! Heh-heh-heh!
It's bliz-zar-ding…the mountain's crawling—
   zu-zu-zu-zu
We're burning burning-ga-ga
A wild hum's droning in the entrails
   GU-GU-GUR

Гудит земля, зудит земля...
     Зудозем... зудозем...
Ребячий и щенячии пупок дискантно вопит:
     У—а—а! У—а—а!...
Собаки и санях застулились
И тысяча беспроволочных зертей
И одна ведзьма под забором плачут:
     ЗА—ХА—ХА — ХА! а—а!
     За—хе—хе—хе!—е!
     ПА—ПА—А—ЛСЯ!!!
     Па—па—а—лся!
Буран растет... высзга зудит...
На кожанный костряк
Вскочил Шаман
     Шаман
Всех запорошил:
Зыз—з—з
Глыз—з—з
Мизиз—з—з
     З—З—З—З!
Шыга...
Цуав...
     Ицив—
ВСЕ СОБАКИ
            СДОХЛИ!

Earth's droning, earth's itching…
  Earthitch earthitch
The bellybutton of kids and puppies is trebly bawling out
  W-a-a! W-a-a! —ah!
Dog in sleighs slumped
And a thousand wireless zatans
And one witzch under the fence are weeping:
  ZA-HA-HA-HA! a-a!
  Za-heh-heh-heh! eh!
  GAH-GAH-AH-TYU!!!
  Gah-gah-ah-tyu!
Blizzard's growing…stormz itching…
Shaman sprang
At the leathery boneton
  Shaman
Powdered everybody
Ziz-z-z-
Eiz-z-z-
Fzorz-z-z-
  Z-Z-Z-Z
Shiga…
Tsuav…
Itseev….
ALL THE DOGS
    CROAKED!

РЕВЮЧЕСТЬ
(Крылышко романа)

Милый
            Дориан-дрянь!
С ужимкой
и часовой цепочкой
            на шарабане
брянцает
            в Рязань.
Сгрязает
            у зашипренной крясавицы
у Акулины Яковлевны
            —акулы!—
(Я ревнюю!.. ревнюю!..)

            Уобляриганенной красавицы,
            полный соблазнов
            любви на колесах
            сигар
            И услады-ды-ды-ды
            гремят серенады-ды-ды

Разлучница
            милого в печке
                        прижала-ла-ла-ла...
...Я ей косыньки все
побледневшею ручкой
                        повыдергиваю-ю-ю-юю!...
Глав—трух...
глав—сплетня...
камнем катится слух...
Старуха подслепая,
язвуха
все перепутала
разгряза-а-а-нила...

JEALOUSIDITY
(a winglette of a novel)

Dear
     Dorian—trash!
With a grimace
and a watchfor
     he clatters
on the gig
     to Ryazan.
Filthies up
     the perfumey bee-youtea
at Akulina Yakovlenna's
     (the shark)
—I'm jealousing!…jealousing!—

     At the ooblatrollopy beauty's
     he's full of the devil,
     of love at the wheel,
     cigars.
     And deligh-ting-ting-ting
     Serenade-nade-nades rumblalong!

The splitress
     nud-nud-nud-nudged
          her lover at the stove…
…*With this paling*
little hand I'll ya-ya-ya-yank
     all her pigtails!
Head-rot,
head-gossip,
hearsay a rolling stone…
The near-sighted hag,
the ulcerrag's
scrambled everything up
smearfil-thi-ly…

—Му-гу-гу-у-у-у!—
к дорогому Дориану побегу.

Прискакаю—
           он сидит
возле печки,
возле кòшачьего хвòста
кудри греет у огня
и ни капельки

           не поедет
           миленочек
           в Рязань...

Грудь промерзла,
к милому люному
доползти не смогу—
—му-гу-гу-у-у!..—
В голос горький замяучу:
—Кровь польется с моей раны
на истоптанный песок,
издивлялся чорный гровон,
чуя лакомый кусок...
           Ох! Ох!
Сонный
           машется
                    платок!..

—I'll ran to dear Dorian…
Moo-goo-goo-oo-oo-oo!

I gallop in.
     He's sitting
by the stove
next to the cat's tail
warming his curls by the fire
and little sweetpie

     ain't budging
     a droplet
     toward Ryazan

Breast frozen through,
I can't even crawl
to my belyublee youthy—
  moo-goo-goo-oo-oo!
I'll miao at the bitter voice:
—Blood's going to flow from my wound
onto the trampled sand;
the black graven was asstounded
scenting a dainty piece…
     Oh, oh!
A sleepy
    shawl's
       flapping!

Alexei Kruchenykh was born to a peasant family near Kherson in 1886. A high school art teacher, he was to abandon painting for poetry, and in 1911 joined the group Hylaea (later to become the Cubo-Futurist movement), whose members included David and Nikolai Burliuk, Benedikt Livshits, Vasily Kamensky, Elena Guro, Velimir Khlebnikov and Vladimir Mayakovsky.

His first books of poetry date from the same year, and were illustrated by the luminaries of the early 20th century Russian avant-garde: Natalya

Goncharova, Mikhail Larionov, Kazimir Malevich, Olga Rozanova and Vladimir Tatlin. Notable among his early works is Pomade (1913), which included "dyr bul shchyl," the first zaum poem. The year 1913 also saw the production of Kruchenykh's opera Victory over the Sun, with music by Mikhail Matyushin and sets and costumes by Malevich, who traced the origins of Suprematism back to this work.

To avoid the draft, Kruchenykh "retired" to the Caucasus in 1916, settling in Tblissi where he quickly became a central figure in a burgeoning avant-garde scene. With Ilya and Kirill Zdanevich and Igor Terentiev, he founded the group 41°, which quickly became one of the most radical of all Russian Futurist groups, promoting their work, mostly zaum poems and plays, in public lectures and readings at a local nightclub. Perhaps the most significant of the Futurist theoreticians and polemicists, Kruchenych provided the theoretical framework for their writing in a series of seminal manifestoes, most of which, like the 1921 "Declaration of Transrational Language," focus specifically on zaum.

His books, which by his own accounts numbered in the hundreds, were works of art in their own right. They were often sloppily produced, using a combination of hand written and rubber stamped texts which were mimeographed on cheap paper of different colors and sizes, a technique that reflected the irreverent, primitive esthetic that informed his poetry, which was replete with blasphemous and scatological imagery, and marred with frequent misspellings and grammatical errors.

In addition to books of poetry, Kruchenykh also wrote a number of interesting theoretical works dealing with sound in language, among them Verbal Texture and Shiftology of Russian Verse (1923), and Phonetics of Theater (1925), as well as a number of studies on the poetry of Esenin.

When Futurism fell out of favor with the Communist Party, Kruchenykh all but disappeared from the Soviet literary scene, publishing virtually nothing after 1934. He was not represented in the literary encyclopedias and reference books of the time, and reportedly went back to teaching art to high school students to earn a living. He died in 1968.

San Francisco poet Jack Hirschman has translated numerous poets from the Russian and other languages.

Amelia Rosselli

from *War Variations*

*Translated from the Italian by Lucia Re
and Paul Vangelisti*

Il soggiorno in inferno era di natura divina
ma le lastre della provvidenza ruggivano nomi
retrogradi e le esperienze del passato si facevano
più voraci e la luna pendeva anch'essa non più
melanconica e le rose del giardino sfiorivano
lentamente al sole dolce. Se sfioravo il giardino
esso mi penetrava con la sua dolcezza nelle ossa
se cantavo improvvisamente il sole cadeva. Non
era dunque la natura divina delle cose che scuoteva
il mio vigoroso animo ma la malinconia.

✳

La mia vita si salvò per un retrograde amore. La mia
vita s'impennò per una lavata di testa. Le mie circostanze
furono tali ch'io non potei scappare dagli altri.
I miei concittadini levavano bandiere e gridi e risollevarono
i cuori. Io dormivo — assaggiavo il sole.

✳

Prendevo la spada e gridavo: fuori di quà cuorleone
che mi hai trafitto il cuore. Prendevo la spada e sbagliavo
o trovavo clientela? Corrotta la gioventù di oggi, corrotto
il mercato corrotta la gente che compra corrotto il mercato
e la mercantilizia. E se il mare geme e la mia fronte è
perlata di sudore? Lagrime in silenzio.

The stay in hell was of a divine nature
but the slabs of providence roared retrograde
names and experiences of the past became more
voracious and the moon hung she too no longer
melancholy and the roses in the garden slowly
died in the sweet sun. If I grazed the garden
it penetrated my bones with its sweetness
if I sang the sun all of a sudden fell. It wasn't
the divine nature of things then that shook
my vigorous soul but the melancholy.

*

My life was saved by a retrograde love. My
life got ruffled for a scolding. My circumstances
were such that I could not escape from others.
My fellow citizens raised flags and screamed and lifted
their hopes. I slept—I tasted the sun.

*

I took the sword and screamed: out of here lionhearted
you have pierced my heart. I took the sword and I was wrong
or did I find a clientele? The youth of today corrupt, corrupt
the market corrupt the people who buy corrupt the marketplace
and the merchant class. And if the sea moans and my forehead is
covered with pearls of sweat? Tears in silence.

Atterrita la signorina sbilanciava sulle nevi dei suoi scì
acquatici. La giornata si pronunciava difficile e arguta:
il sole subentrava molto glorioso ma fuori delle finestre
nevicava un ingenuo candore che lei non teneva fra le braccia!
del suo desiderio. Desiderava cose impossibili: amicizia
e fedeltà. Cercava sorridente la prova della sua malizia:
lei stessa carpiva,—od era trattenuta dalla gente? Malizia
che imperi nel mio sangue violaceo di violetta abbandonata
io ti perdono: ma muore il cuore. La gioventù corrotta
sorgeva abbandonando il suo posto. Lei mirava ad un fine
più stabile: trovava polvere e pipistrelli e formicaioli
e donnaioli sul suo cammino di erbe basse. Sotto al suo
piede si fermava la luce.

(Nel cuore della notte tremava la luce.) Tramava cose impossibili!
Cercava la notte che schiudeva i suoi petali nell'ignoto.

Rimasi per terra e caddi supina.

I bambini d'inferno crescevano sporadicamente, le
tue acquerella scomponevano la mia mente. O acque
forti da deglutare: o canzone preferita che ti sei
rivelata canzonetta da radio-trattoria. La traiettoria
dei razzi precisi è più vera di tutta la tua pretesa
del bello e del buono e del rotatorio. Ruota intorno
a me senza colpo ferire: io parto per la luna. È
partito il vicino più grande di me, io lo seguo.

Terrified the young lady was losing her balance on the snow of her
water skis. The day pronounced itself difficult and witty:
the sun took over very gloriously but outside the windows
it was snowing a naive honesty she didn't hold in the arms!
of her desire. She desired impossible things: friendship
and faithfulness. Smiling she looked for proof of his malice:
she herself snatched—or was she held up by people? Malice
you who rule in my violet blood of an abandoned violet
I forgive you: but the heart dies. The corrupt youth
rose abandoning its place. She yearned for a more stable
end. She discovered dust and bats and anteaters
and womanizers along her way of low grasses. Under
her foot the light stopped.

(In the heart of the night light trembled.) Plotting impossible things!
Looking for the night that opened her petals in the unknown.

I remained on the ground and fell on my back.

*

The children of hell grew sporadically, your
watercolors decomposed my mind. O strong
waters to swallow: o favorite song that revealed
itself a tune from the radio-diner. The trajectory
of the precise rockets is truer than all your pretense
of the beautiful and the good and the circular. Circle
me without striking a blow: I leave for the moon. The
neighbor bigger than me has left, I follow him.

*The daughter of an Italian father and an English mother, Rosselli was born
in Paris in 1930, and spent her childhood in France. Growing up speaking*

French, English and Italian, Rosselli was, from her childhood on, multilingual, which, in turn, would highly influence the syntactical complexity of her poetry.

Another determining factor of her life was the murder of her father, the anti-Fascist martyr Carlo and her uncle, Nelo Rosselli—both brutally killed by order of Benito Mussolini and Galaeazzo Ciano at Bagnole-de-l'Orne in Normandy. This event and its aftermath—during the war she and her mother traveled throughout Europe to escape the Nazis—would have lasting effects on her mental health. Much of her life was spent in therapy, and in 1996 she leaped from her high-rise apartment to her death. Rosselli herself has described the death of her father as leaving an emotional void which she attempted to fill through her writing.

After the war, she and her mother returned to Italy, staying for a short while in Florence before moving by herself to England, where she studied music: violin, piano, and composition. The following year, after the death of her mother, Rosselli was forced, at the age of eighteen, to find self-employment. She began as a translator for Communità in Rome. And here, directed by her father's cousin, Alberto Pincherli (the prominent Italian novelist Alberto Moravia), she began reading Italian writers while continuing to study music. She also met, during these years, the Italian poet Rocco Scotellaro, a resistance partisan, who would remain her friend until his early death in 1953.

Among her several books are Viariazioni belliche (War Variations), which will be published in English by Sun & Moon Press in 1998, Serie ospedaliera (1969), Documento, 1996-1732 (1976), Impromptu (1981) and Appunti sparsi e persi (1983).

Paul Vangelisti is the editor of Ribot, co-editor of Littoral Press, and former editor of Red Hill Press. He is the author of many works of poetry, including Nemo, Another You, A Life, and Villa. He has translated extensively from the Italian. His translation of Adriano Spatola's Collected Poems will be published by Sun & Moon Press.

Lucia Re teaches at the University of California, Los Angeles. She has written extensively on Italian modernism.

José Antonio Mazzotti

Two Poems

Translated from the Spanish by G. J. Racz

Y estás viéndola de nuevo, sus ojos fatigados, sus manitas
cogiendo en cualquier parte su puño de tierra.
Vientorepugnante que sostiene su cuerpo y lo empuja!

Una silla en el banco su destino / acostumbrada
a roer los esfínteres del diablo, Pancha (para los amigos)
bebe una y otra vez whisky on the rocks.
Y es una sola sombra larga,
Y es una sola sombra larga,
Y es una sola sombra larga cuando se desnuda en el verano
como una fruta chillando tras la cáscara roja.
"Clases de marketing los sábados, querido; los domingos
hacia el sur", y sus días van poniendo una a una
las piedras de su casa en la ciudad.

Todos sabemos su historia: la encontraron
besando en la cama un bello fantasma. Su marido
(un padre ofidio y cordial) le señaló con la espada el resto del
camino.

Y es una sola sombra larga, Francesca, cuando mira
sobre el mar las alas verdes, azules, amarillas
de los pájaros flotando hacia otro mundo.
Empina su cerveza y seca el frasco:
                                        un catovit, dos catovit,
            tres catovit, son su pasaje favorito.
Ella también lo sabe, pero no se apura.
Francesca, mujer de 21 años, se deja arrastrar por el viento
de roca en roca y de pared en pared.

Su cadáver despierta todavía
el deseo de los transeúntes.

You are seeing her again for the very first time, the tired eyes, the
        tiny hands
scraping up a fistful of dirt wherever she can find one.
A repulsivewind sustains her body, propelling it forward!

A seat on the bench her destiny, accustomed to
gnawing the devil's asshole, Frannie (to her friends)
drinks one scotch on the rocks after another.
And she is just a long shadow,
Just a long shadow,
Just a long shadow when she strips naked in the summer
like a fruit shrieking behind its red peel.
"Business class on Saturdays, darling; on Sundays
I travel south." Her days move the stones of her house
one by one into the city.

We all know the story: found kissing
a handsome ghost in bed. Her husband
(a snake-like, cordial father) pointed out the rest of the way with
        his sword.

And she is just a long shadow, Francesca is, when above the sea
she watches the green, blue and yellow wings
of birds floating off to another world.
She tips her bottle and drains the beer:
                                one pep pill, two pep pills,
        three pep pills—they are her favorite trip.
She knows it, too, but does not worry.
Francesca, a woman twenty-one years of age, lets herself be
        dragged by the wind
from rock to rock and wall to wall.

Her corpse still arouses
desire in passersby.

¿Demasiada soberbia no resulta
detener lo que el viento por costumbre
arrastra atravesando bosques, hilvanando
su orden al nuestro con la geometría
de los astros?

Ahora por la orilla del río deambulas
y sólo te mereces el instante que allí gozas:
repetir será siempre un regalo, pero nunca
el mismo. Solamente la acción que se repite
nos inflama: si en piedra queremos convertirla
no hay río, si queremos
parar también el viento
qué pobre inflamación la que nos queda.
Y Llama de Amor Viva, que murmura,
qué poco es el consuelo y sin embargo
qué terca la paciencia de encontrar sentido
a trozos de granito sobre el mundo en blanco.

Tus pies sobre la arena,
las gotas en la hierba,
el llanto de las aguas repetidas:
humildad con que olvidas el tormento
de aislarte aislándolos
cual joven cazador que sólo encuentra
placer en el cadáver de los ciervos.

Does not overweening pride end up
holding back what the wind habitually
drags away, crossing forests, threading
its order into ours with the geometry
of the stars?

Now you stroll along the riverbank
and only deserve the moment you enjoy there:
repeating this will always be a gift, yet never
the same one. Only repeat action
rouses our flames: should we wish to convert it to stone
there will be no river; should we wish to
stop the wind,
what a sorry arousal will remain!
Flame of Burning Love amurmur,
how small the consolation and yet
how dogged one's patience must be to find meaning
in chunks of granite above a blank world.

Your feet upon the sand,
the raindrops on the grass,
the wail of repeating waters:
humility with which you forget the torment
of isolating yourself by isolating these things
like a young hunter who finds his only
pleasure in the corpses of deer.

José Antonio Mazzotti was born in Lima, Peru in 1961. He began writing poetry as early as the age of twelve, and was a member of the Generation of '80, *a group of young poets who strove to integrate into their work the conflicting identities comprising Peruvian society. Mazzotti's poetic reputation was established early in his native land when he received the* Premio Nacional

Universitario *for his first collection of verse,* Poemas no recogidos en libro *(Poems Uncollected) in 1980. Four years later, he published* Fierro curvo *(Curved Iron), a departure from the more conventional disquisitions on love and poetry of his first volume. Here he developed his talent for the colloquial narrative techniques dominant in Latin American poetry. In 1988 Mazzotti was a finalist for the* Premio de Poesía Casa de las Américas, *and the following year he published a selection of poems,* Castillo de popa *(Roundhouse). Currently a co-editor of a series of chapbooks of Spanish-language poetry,* Tabla/de poesía actual, *Mazzotti has just completed work on two additional volumes of verse,* Parque de los demonios *(Park of Devils) and* Libro de las Auroras Boreales *(Northern Lights). Both of these works concern themselves with a vision of Peruvian myth and history that refashion national character and identity.*

G. J. Racz teaches Spanish translation at Rutgers University. He has translated numerous works, including Benito Pérez Galdós's novel Gerona, *work by Andalusian poet José Manuel del Pino, Mazzotti, Eduardo Chirinos, and selections of Argentine experimental writers of the* Xul *group, published in 1998 by Roof Books.*

Eduardo Chirinos

Pirata de la memoria / Pirate of Memory

Translated from the Spanish by G. J. Racz

Voici l'écumeur de mémoire
—RENÉ CHAR

El tiempo de los caídos en combate,
el tiempo de los ánsares en celo, el tiempo
del hacha enmohecida por la lluvia
me hunde en una triste sucesión de olvidos.
Hablo del tiempo que empaña la memoria y así la purifica,
de antiguos balcones que resbalan hacia el mar,
de siniestras florecillas que devoran los pelícanos en tiempos
    de hambre ye de miseria.

Hablo de la estrella roja y de la estrella blanca.
Del día que concebí un hijo entre desechos y animales mutilados,
del sol que abrasó dos cuerpos fulgurantes
y luego se detuvo para dar paso a la noche.
Hablo del amor que refulge como un trozo de vidrio ahumado
    por la sangre,
vidrio remoto donde arden águilas y hienas como en un lecho nupcial.

Hablo de la muerte del amor y del renacimiento del amor,
de pechos taraceados por la rabia,
de largas agonías sin plegarias ni arrepentimientos.
Hablo también de lluvias y naufragios,
del hijo que asesinó a su padre una noche de tormenta
y enloqueció en plazas inmundas y lejanísimos puertos.

…

Hablo de la estrella roja y de la estrella blanca.
Nada ganaré con recordarlo, salvo el dolor de recordarlo;
la vana pasión que recorre mis días no se parece al sueño
ni la vejez al soportable rencor de los sentidos.
Vuelo sin alas, escupo en el barro, hojeo amarillos volúmenes
    donde otros han escrito lo que yo he de escribir
y no obtengo respuesta.

The time of those fallen in battle,
the time of geese in heat, the time
of the ax rusted in the rain
sets me on the sad course of forgetting.
I am talking about time that purifies memory by blurring it,
about ancient balconies slipping into the sea,
about sinister little flowers the pelicans devour in times of
    hunger and hardship.

I am talking about the red star and the white.
About the day I conceived a child among scraps of garbage and
    mutilated animals,
about the sun that scorched two sleek bodies
and then stopped to give way to the night.
I am talking about love that shines like a piece of glass made
    cloudy by blood,
remote glass where eagles and hyenas burn as in a marriage bed.

I am talking about the death of love and its rebirth,
about bosoms inlaid with rage,
about long bouts in death's throes without prayers or repentance.
I am talking about rains and shipwrecks, too,
about the son who killed his father one stormy night
and later went mad in filthy public squares and far-off ports.

…

I am talking about the red star and the white.
I'll gain nothing by remembering this except the pain of remembering;
the empty passion that runs through my days and no more resembles sleep
than old age the tolerable resentment of the senses.
I fly without wings, spit in the mud, flip through yellowed volumes
    where others have written what I am to write,
but I receive no reply.

Nada poseo sino la palabra,
el resto lo he perdido en el naufragio de los días.
Nada poseo sino la palabra,
la palabra que ahora se escabulle dejándome solo.

I possess nothing but the word,
having lost the rest in the shipwreck of my days.
I possess nothing but the word,
the word now slipping away, leaving me on my own.

Eduardo Chirinos was born in Lima in 1960, and studied at the Universidad Católica, where he received his undergraduate degree in Humanities and a Master's in Hispanic Literatures. He returned to teach in the Universidad Católica's Department of Humanities before coming to America to obtain his doctorate in Spanish from Rutgers University.

Chirinos is the author of eight books of poetry: Cuadernos de Horacio Morell *(Horacio Morell's Notebooks) (Lima, 1981);* Crónicas de un ocioso *(Chronicles of a Man of Leisure) (Lima, 1983);* Archivo de huellas digitales *(Fingerprint File) (Lima, 1986);* Sermón sobre la muerte *(Sermon on Death) (Madrid, 1986);* Rituales del conocimiento y del sueño *(Rituals of Knowledge and Dream) (Madrid, 1987);* El libro de los encuentros *(The Book of Encounters) (Lima, 1988);* Canciones del Herrero del Arca *(Songs of the Ark's Blacksmith) (Lima, 1989), and* Recuerda, cuerpo... *(Remember, Body...) (Madrid, 1991). Recently his selected works were published in Mexico as* Raritan Blues, *and a ninth volume,* El equilibrista de Bayard Street *(The Bayard Street Tightrope Walker) is at press.*

In addition to his poetry, Chirinos has published a book of essays and has edited two volumes of verse.

Ishihara Yoshirô

Three Poems
Translated from the Japanese by Hiroaki Sato

CONDITIONS

Conditions are given   from a bat's ears
to a sunset fountain
because of conditions
we get up, lie down
because of conditions
we are mopped up all at once
but as for the most cruel conditions
there is still another   and
only one
what you can seek from me and can't get
a nose-like ear
a foot-like hand
for this day is breathing hot
within conditions
and further the day that follows
therefore   we
stop walking
desperately inclining
toward a hot, brilliant thing
that's rising to the cheeks to the sky
like blood   abruptly

ACCEPTANCE

Got it? That's what
acceptance is all about.
It may be
something like a flag.
It may be
something like a suppressed breath
When it is something like a flag
a merchant will be sharply distinguished
from a wind.
When it is something like a suppressed
breath
you need only a small voice
barely audible.
Or it may be
something like a barrel,
may be
something like evidence.
You suddenly turn your eyes down,
slowly drop your
stubborn jaw.
Whether death is before you
or a horse cart is before you
that's what acceptance is
all about.
Throwing down the reasons that smell of leather
the old man sobs,
the boy urinates.
Whether you crouch
or walk off
the unshaven defense
ends there.

FACT

What is there
is there
as is.
Look,
a hand is there,
a foot is there,
it's even snickering.
If you've seen it,
say you've seen it.
Each time with a clatter
you step on a cup, crushing it,
push open the door,
and hurry off, placed
flat on your back of countless
humiliations
a thick palm.
Where are you running to?
Even if every one of them
disappears,
it's there,
it is there as is.
Like a criminal whose punishment is forgotten,
look,
a foot is there,
a hand is there,
and
it's even snickering.

Ishihara Yoshirô was imprisoned while serving in Manchuria during World War II, and indicted by the Soviet Union after the war of anti-Soviet activities and sentenced to twenty-five years of hard labor. Throughout the late 1940s, he worked with Romanian, German, and Russian "criminals" in for-

est-clearing along the Baikal-Amur Railroad. In 1950, he was moved to Khabarovsk, from where, after Stalin's death, he was released.

His first book of poetry, Sancho Pansa no Kikyô, *did not appear until 1963. His selected poems appeared in 1967, which included works from some of his poems and essays. His last book, a selection of tanka, was published after his death in 1977. Sun & Moon Press will publish a selection of his works, titled* Funeral Train and Other Poems, *which includes works from* Sancho Pansa no Kikyô, Ichimai no Uwagi no Uta, Ono no Shisô *and his tanka.*

One of the most noted translators of Japanese literature, Hiroaki Sato has translated the poetry of Miyazawa Kenji, Takahashi Mutsuo, Yoshioka Minoru, Hagiwara Sakutaro, and others. He was awarded the P.E.N. Award in translation, with Burton Watson, for their The Country of Eight Islands *in 1982. Sun & Moon Press will publish his translation of the poems of Hagiwara in 1998.*

Benjamin Péret

The Four Elements
from *Natural History*
Translated from the French by Guy Bennett

EARTH

The world is made of water, earth, air and fire and the earth is not round but bowl-shaped. It is a heavenly breast whose twin stands in the middle of the milky way.

The earth breeds flies, diurnal spirits appointed to protect it in hot weather for, in cold weather, the earth dries out, becomes a gourd and no longer needs a guard, while in summer smoke comes out of its ears and, without the flies to guide it up into the air, clouds would lie about the earth like filthy rags.

When watered, earth gives:

1. Lipstick from which kisses are extracted.

There are two types of lipsticks: undulating, long-wave lipstick which, when distilled, gives flags, and light lipstick whose flower produces kisses. These kisses can be obtained in two ways, either by drying the flower plucked at the moment it blooms, or by crushing its seed which gives a highly volatile essence that is difficult to preserve.

2. The Turkish bath, which is obtained by kneading moist earth with curdled milk and makes so much noise that it has been gradually relegated to deserted regions.

3. The frog, which slowly devours the earth.

4. The cello, used more and more frequently in treating arthritis and, ground to a powder, enjoys great favor in the washing of delicate fabrics as it doesn't affect the color.

5. Glasses for the near-sighted, which are obtained by softening a little earth in a boiling infusion of China tea, then setting the mixture to cook in a double boiler.

A great many other things are extracted from moist earth as well, like the compass, the saveloy, the boxer, the match, the preposition, etc... that our grandmothers were still using but which can only be found today in antique shops.

By blowing on earth, that is by mixing it with air, you get the gooseberry if you blow lightly, if you blow violently, you get the tricycle.

The use of mechanical processes (whose origins will be discussed later) which allow one to insufflate the earth with greater quantities of air, has bred the sieve, obtained by forcing a powerful jet of air kept at room temperature into a pile of earth stained with chicken droppings. Clay, when reduced to dust and placed in a receptacle whose air, circulated by a powerful fan, goes from the point of freezing to fifty degrees above zero and vice versa every five minutes, gives the concierge. Invented by Albert the Great, it has since been perfected but is worn out more quickly now than in the past.

In a receptacle containing air at a pressure of three atmospheres and subjected to very low temperatures, earth gives the knitting needle. Increasing the pressure and lowering the temperature, you get the blackbird, the cradle, the pea and the horrible motorcycle.

In thin, toasted slices, earth becomes a fishhook, in thick slices singed on a roaring fire it becomes a urinal; rolled into balls and exploding in the fire it gives the grasshopper and, if the ball is large, the mustache.

AIR

Air, in its normal state, secretes a steady cloud of pepper that makes the earth sneeze. On the ground, the pepper condenses until it gives the knick-knack in summer and the newspaper in winter. By simply placing the latter in a cool place it turns into a railway station or a sponge, depending on the number of pages. The pepper also condenses at a height of two thousand meters, then falls back to earth in a powder so fine that no one notices it, but the testament to such flagrant uselessness eventually appears as, unbeknownst to them, passers-by inevitably trample it. At greater heights, the pepper nourishes the stars, giving them their luster.

Painted blue, air makes undergrowth in dry weather; in rainy weather it makes bleach, but is then harmful to man who absorbs large doses of it for it causes ulcers, boils, and damages tooth enamel. Painted yellow, air is used to dress furs and, mixed with powder of cockchafer, cures lockjaw. When sucked on, air is used to repair innertubes, when salted, it becomes a bed. Warmed between the hands, it dilates to the point of changing into a whip. Torn to shreds and sprinkled with red wine, it gives the maestro, so useful to peasants at harvest time. Dried in the sun and preserved all winter in a dry place, in spring air will give the engagement ring which, due to its extreme sensitivity to variations in temperature, is very fragile and rarely reaches maturity.

Shut up in a closet, air tends to escape so as to blow out the door at the first possibility, taking the shape of a mushroom generally used today to fight wrinkles.

Pickled in vinegar, air gives the porter which, in windy weather, is as runny as overripe cheese. The runny porter is then collected, dried, carefully ground and then sown in a shady spot. Within a month the moon sprouts, emerges from the earth and blooms, for the moon is not a heavenly body as is generally believed, but the pollen of countless female runny porter-flowers that rises every evening, whereas the male flowers fall to the ground leaving their seed to sprout again. Every morning the moon plunges into the sea and, as it hits the waves, produces the tides. As it dissolves, the moon gives the sea its salty taste.

WATER

In the form of rain, water becomes an earthworm as it penetrates the soil. These earthworms, reaching great depths, gather in countless masses in natural cavities and produce petroleum by spitting. There are several types of petroleum:

1. Hobnailed petroleum which has but a brief existence for it is eaten by moths.

2. Petroleum beans favored by elephants because it stimulates the growth of their tusks.

3. Unicorn petroleum which, as petroleum, is useless. Only its horn, eroded by the wind, gives birth to the marathon runner, which is constantly used in the porcelain industry for the purification of the kaolin that must first be purged with squid ink administered in large doses.

4. Hoarse petroleum, so called because of the inelegant sounds it emits. That's where we get the bells that spread the germs of infectious diseases.

5. Hairy petroleum, which attaches itself to the bark of trees in cold countries and, eventually, gives sparrow eggs, firecrackers and pins, in that order. When the firecrackers and pins mate they give birth to red billiard balls which terrify carp. Their ferocity is such that within a few days, the most abundant fishponds become barren and the red ball dies of hunger shortly thereafter, producing will-o'-the-wisps in the process.

6. Snowy petroleum, which is found only on the highest mountains of Europe. Above two thousand meters, this type of petroleum loses its qualities, tarnishes, becomes brittle and, if left in the sun, turns into a chair, a harmless looking lemur whose highly venomous bite can be fatal if not treated promptly.

River water, in moonlight, gives the hen whose feathers are much sought after in the production of low coastlines. In summer, the hens have no feathers but are bristling with red teeth which, when ground, are used to make candles, so useful in the countryside to detect the presence of water tables. These waters are inhabited by multitudes of keys which, as soon as a well is sunk, escape through the opening and fly off to nest on the tops of tall trees to the sound of their shrill cries. After nightfall, they band together and attack dogs that flee at their approach, baying at the moon.

Having risen to ground level, well water evaporates quickly, leaving a beautiful light green residue at the bottom of the receptacle: the principle of causality, which, soluble in oil, is the father of the artichoke. When heated, well water hardens, dilates, and acquires, at a temperature of eighty degrees, a great elasticity which makes it susceptible to becoming a kangaroo within a few days. But this kangaroo is prey to respiratory illnesses, not to mention tuberculosis which has destroyed great numbers of them as well. That's why the deadwood kangaroo, which is much more robust than the others, is preferred by rabbit breeders whose products, at its very contact, acquire a long, silky coat, which is highly prized in the production of flags. When the temperature drops below zero, well water turns into a beggar which, sliced wafer-thin, is used in the production of grottos.

When sea water evaporates, it gives a bristle whose longevity is truly astonishing. There have been reports of thousand year old female bristles that still give birth every year to four litters of shot glasses, and each litter is made up of a dozen glasses… One can easily imagine that, in these conditions, the shot glass would have become, for man, a scourge worse than plagues of locusts had it not found a fierce enemy in the crutch. Indeed, each crutch annually devours tens of thousands of shot glasses and, in equatorial Africa alone, crutches, of which there are some twenty species, gather in countless flocks which, having devoured all the shot glasses they can find, begin to terrorize the natives, destroying their crop of calf's liver, thus reducing them to a state of poverty and famine.

Finally, there is also bearded water, about which little is known (it is used to make suits of armor favored by shivery old women), flying water, with which navigators plot their position, light water, from which swimming trunks are extracted, hardwood water, indispensable to confectioners, dusty water, used in carpentry, feathery water, hunted in December when its feathers take on their brightest colors, cinder water, used in electricity, and many others that will be discussed later.

FIRE

An essentially mineral element, fire resides in stones and eggs. When damp and left in the sun, quivering stones give the best fire, velvety-smooth and fragrant, popular in the burning of churches; but they mustn't quiver too much for, if their quivering is too pronounced, fire melts, giving us tartar sauce whose needles, pricking anyone who touches it, inoculate him with begonias which makes the person yawn from morning to night. If the stone quivers inter- mittently, the fire coughs and spits a damp moss that extinguishes it, giving birth to fleas dreaded by dry cleaners for the damage they do to colored dyes. Disturbed by the presence of fleas, colored dyes lose their brilliance, so much so in fact that it is impossible to achieve a uniform color. On the other hand, this disruptive action is prized by those dry cleaners seeking to produce a marbled effect. They simply place equal parts of both fleas and coloring agent in a closed container and keep the mixture at a high temperature, for a more or less lengthy period, depending on whether they wish to obtain marbling or moiré.

Left out in the rain all winter, windy stones give a blazing, but short-lived fire if care is not taken to soak these stones in the sea before using them, that is before putting them in a reed cage that favors the production of fire. The fire then attracts moles which it feeds on and which thus contribute to the increase of both its dura- tion and intensity.

A great many types of fire are known. Among the most popular are thin sliced fire from which bottles are extracted which, set to soak in a quinine bath, give in turn a fire so hard that special tools are necessary to saw it into boards so sturdy and light that children make kites out of them. There is also clog fire, offspring of the sleeping car and the wheelbarrow, which is prized by composers for, stretched out on a soft bed and well-dressed, it emits, once it has been lightly salted, the symphony and, sprinkled with ink, the opera. One of the more common fires, the reeking fire, is obtained by steeping a bishop in cod liver oil. It gives off a foul odor, but facilitates the cultivation of asparagus, for reeking fire destroys the filecabinets that begin gnawing away at them as soon as they break soil. We should also mention cloud fire which keeps mice and rats from moving into uninhabited houses, muslin fire, indispensable in baking, austrich fire, that all young women slip into their cor- sages the night of their first dance, limping fire, terror of doctors for it causes epidemics (as soon as it appears it is fought off with leek spray), beaten fire, which disturbs sleeping villagers the night before the harvest, stick fire, pill fire, powdered fire, dry fire, black and white fire, striped fire, doctoral fire, etc.

All of these fires can be readily found anywhere in the world in a more or less pure state, but they can be easily cleaned, either with fish bones, or by passing them through filter paper soaked in vinegar. There are, however, still other, rarer types of fire — button fire, for example, that goes so well on blondes, brain fire that is produced with great difficulty by pounding turkeys with couchgrass until you get a thick paste that you set out to dry in the sun after dusting it with equal quantities of finely ground iron and copper filings. If the filings are not fine enough, the paste runs and gives pennies, if they are too fine, birds peck at the paste which soon explodes in a cloud of black dust that sticks to your skin and that can only be washed off with a tincture of iodine. With one kilo of this paste, you get a knob of brain fire which is extracted from the dried paste by breaking it open. But you must take care not to drop it onto wool, which would become rabid. Folded in turn, brain fire, mixed with ground heliotrope flowers, is prepared like tea and given to women who wish to have beauty marks. Among the rare fires, let us also note shutter fire, which seeps out of volcanic ash long after the eruption, at the rate of a few grams per ton of ash treated with cider, it is indeed quite rare; jowl fire, used as an ornamental motif, flying fire, forbidden in milliners' studios for it turns the employees against their bosses; rose fire, that can be found in the woods in springtime, very early in the morning; crossbow fire, which is a very rare illness affecting snails (one in ten thousand is stricken); shivering fire; suspender fire; breast fire; and finally crumb fire, which is occasionally secreted by the female penguin while laying eggs, but which evaporates very quickly if not immediately collected in sour cream.

Author of some fifteen collections of poetry, a novel, a natural history, more than thirty short stories, a pornographic farce, numerous theoretical and political tracts; editor of two anthologies, co-editior (with Pierre Naville) of La Révolution surréaliste, *and co-author of Breton, Éluard, and Desnos,*

Benjamin Péret remains one of the most prolific, yet least known of the major surrealist writers.

Born on July 4, 1899, Péret, like many of his future colleagues, fought in the first world war. He moved to Paris in 1920, determined to make a career for himself as a writer. At a gathering for the dada journal Littérature, Péret met André Breton, Louis Aragon, and Paul Éluard, and began to participate in their activities. His first book of poetry, Le passager du transatlantique was published the following year with illustrations by Hans Arp.

Numerous other publications followed, among them Au 125 boulevard Saint-Germain with illustrations by Max Ernst (1923), 152 proverbes mis au goût du jour with Éluard (1925), and Dormir, dormir dans les pierres, illustrated by Yves Tanguy (1927).

In 1929 Péret left Paris for Brazil. A revolutionary communist, he was imprisoned for his political activity and deported in 1931. Back in France, he organized with Breton the international surrealist exhibition in the Canary Islands in 1935, then left for Spain where joined P.O.U.M. in their fight against Franco. During this time Péret wrote three seminal collections of poetry, Je ne mange pas de ce pain-là, Je sublime (again, with illustrations by Ernst), and Trois cerises et une sardine, the latter being published upon his return to Paris in 1937.

Mobilized at the outset of the second world war, Péret was quickly arrested by the nazis and imprisoned, but released upon the surrender of French forces in 1940. That same year he left France for Mexico, where he would live for eight years, writing Les malheurs d'un dollar (1942), Dernier malheur, dernière chance (1945), and Feu central (1947—illustrated by Tanguy).

Shortly after his return to Paris, Péret wrote his first and only novel La brebis galante (1949—illustrations by Ernst), which was followed by, among other works, the collections Air Mexicain (1952) and Mort aux vaches et au champ d'honneur (1953). In 1955 Péret once again set out for Brazil, living with Indian tribes in the Amazon rain forest, and collecting material for his Anthologie des mythes, légendes et contes populaires d'Amérique published posthumously, one year after his death in Paris on September 18, 1959.

Guy Bennett lives in Los Angeles. He teaches French at UCLA, sets type for Sun & Moon Press, and works as a free lance translator and graphic designer. Recent translations include work by Henri Deluy, Mohammed Dib, and Giovanna Sandri. He edits Seeing Eye Books, a chapbook series devoted to contemporary international poetry. His first book of poems, Last Words, was recently published by Sun & Moon Press.

Marcelin Pleynet
Dogana
Translated from the French by Serge Gavronsky

> *Look at the object without disdain and find*
> *That the eyes who do finally go blind.*
> —ANGELUS SILESIUS

Dazzled

    blind

        turning in the gilded cage of the world

eyes burned by a distant light

           and once more embarked

on the expanse

      hunting in the sky

           here I see this powder

those myriad yellow and luminous thoughts divided they come
settle on the earth where they expect nothing

           I have come back

on my back mouth open

      (it seemed to me I was being called

but no

    I was alone

I was lost

I had just arrived

on this shore

without a doubt one could hear friendly voices calling

should one go

should one stay

should one be modern

what for

and everything I have ever written, felt, lived, held me back
then nothing

silence on the expanse

fear on the other side
all that clutter in the sciences
all those muted books

how to get out
how to quit that pass
how to pass

Suddenly

I thought everything was over for me, all that history
and all those moderns

and all those whys

evoking old Ezra sitting on the steps of the Dogana I thought
that everything begins anew differently like water striking the dock

> "we can see arbitrary caprices in the innumerable
> curves, undulations and breaks in these waves,
> but all of that is necessary, the least backwash
> is mathematically calculable."

Yet again in Venice

        alone

           happy facing that expanse

     I come up against my past
everything has been written down and contradicted

                       happiness

                         truth

      it's no longer the way one thinks

On the page the letters still tremble in front of my eyes
they move not in the way I wish but in the way they wish to be

nothing works anymore in the mind and in books
a single book no longer suffices
meander of thought mathematically incalculable

          in the transparent air
                    I see day flowering
where I shall be alone without possible error
                every man deserves that

as he deserves the error confusing him

today I can recognize every man every book
every living form

                    the long bony stem extending from the base of
the cranium to the posterior section of the trunk

error like truth is upright universal in its meditation

I am familiar with every thought
                    and I move forward painfully in the cleft of time

here at the edge of the Dogana
        between the Palazzo Ducale
                                    and the Church of San Giorgio

        an empty passage on the liquid expanse
                and a spring wind blowing

further
        on the calm sea
                    a sailboat on fire

Suddenly the walls tumble down
                                books
                                    whole sections
the whole library engulfed
                        burned by the luminous light
of letters
        small living letters freeing themselves from the magma

my whole history engulfed
                              burned by luminous letters

life's small living letters jostling each other
                              freed from the magma

guided on the expanse toward the pass
        through innumerable pages where letters run aground
        evoking old Ezra who may actually be the last modern
        and who is not alone in accumulating those ruins through which
        poetry passes

Literally we are not alone
                              but how to free ourselves

what stilled suspicion hovers over the water's expanse
                              all those books…

I see them again in a book
                      on paper

or the letter

what travels within myself far from myself
                                        or too near
              in the West
                        still searching for books
                                        accompanied

what music on the letters
what letter
        what music of being
                        whistles in the spring air

travels
        in the end time and space no longer count

Time and space no longer count

mid-noon/midnight
                a mid-noon tree burns in the blood
                              ideogram where
the column of numbers in profile murmurs on the dock

great wind

            "where men and demons switch roles
             truth and falsehood are confounded"

a boat crosses the lagoon
                 I must relieve myself

far behind
        history
        centuries of great pith
        factories of memory
        the library
        museums
        canning works
        conversations
                far from the ruins of the mind

Who passes with me above the water
how can I be at once in the sky and on the page

what letter holds me back
or am I trapped once again

what letters weave web the image and the thought of the world like a
    trap
like a conspiracy

they call out to me
                come
                     listen to us
                             yesterday we were wrong again

          what joy!

A mid-noon tree burns in the blood
                       it's not me

Homer
        Dante they are not me
                what speaks to me
                a perfume come from the horizon
to the edge of the steps
            in this airy time
                  floating on this violet water
like truth I am there
        but it's not me

he is
I've just thought of it
        I'm there but it's not me

Hölderlin
        why is it said he was mad for forty years

Homer
        why is it said he was blind

that I was mad in its room
that I was blind
                    but it wasn't him

they held dear that thought which assembles
                            which considers thought

the body
        in a certain manner
                        the eyes
                            the labyrinths of the brain

the universe
            the world
                    if one insists
                            in a certain manner

On the dock the old man will soon be two thousand years old

soon three thousand years for old Homer
for young Homer ten thousand years

I'm there
        but it's not me

I think more often about him than I do about myself

Beyond the Aegean Sea waves come to beat against the dock
mathematically calculable even here if you wish
                            depth and expanse and in
                            the pass the goddess Athena
                            with her blue green eyes
                                        that paint
                                        that pain

always present in the letter
                    meander of thought

I'm there

          it's not me

                    I value that sapphire passing in the letter
today once more as it was three thousand years ago

living letters of thought fixed in the heart of the letter
                                        dismissed

speech
          the mind beating against the dock
          pollen
                    powder
                              music in curves

          undulation when the wave breaks
                                        seaspray

inscription
          powder in the golden air
                    in the immediate light contaminated

contaminated blood
                    everything is contaminated
                                        thought itself

history of blood
                    genetic heritage
                              history of thought

suddenly three thousand years behind the eyes
                                        dazzled

intimate conviction
                    action passes in the sun
                                        speed of thought

voices girding the earth

                        the envelope of truth

there are only bodies
                        there are no bodies

there are no bodies where there are only bodies

An empty island   in the distance
                                the sacred envelope of truth

                                the empty envelope of truth in the high sun

on the roofs centuries are present   perfumed
                                Homer   Dante   Villon   Shakespeare

truth and the gift as if I were there
                                truth and goodness

tomorrow 2000 years
                    truth and goodness
                    the cross for the letter
                    Christ ressuscitated in a transparent body as if I were there

in the beginning was color
                              then the letter in the dance of being

ressuscitated in a transparent body as if I were there
                                                  history's end

I have seen these things and seen them with my own eyes seen

my ears have heard

I see
I hear on the liquid ocean the carcass of a boat singing

books burn as if I were there on the page
                                        if I had read them

there is always something rising between men and the transparent
being in flames
                        angering for truth
                        a massacre
                        a column of plaints
                        cities
                        countryside
                        monuments

                    what does not speak of the one to the other

                        churches
                        stone speaking nevertheless
                        marble on the water

            here
                    Palladio facades

the Redentore
San Giorgio

you alone, Christianity, are not prehistoric

but where are the ancients the clever ones among the moderns

facades now burn in front of my eyes
the tree of the flowers of evil burns in negation   letter by letter

and I ask myself why
                    now that an enormous laughter embraces the world

like those waves
                embarked
                            one's got to laugh in their wake

                            now one's got to laugh

Reprinted with permission of the author, from Marcelin Pleynet, *La Dogana* (Paris: Claude Letessier Editeur, 1994).

Marcelin Pleynet was born in 1933 in Lyons. He is a poet, novelist, critic, and art historian. He has written ten volumes of poetry, the most recent of which is, Le propre du temps *(Gallimard, 1995). He has also written two novels and five volumes of his journal, as well as a seminal analysis of Lautréamont and his work on de Sade. He is now concluding two works to appear in the immediate future:* Vuillard *and* La peinture française au xxe siècle. *Pleynet was formerly associate editor of the critical journal* Tel Quel *(1962-1982) and now holds the same position for* L'Infini. *In 1987, he was appointed to the Chair of Aesthetics at the Ecole Nationale Supérieure des Beaux-Arts in Paris. He has lectured in the United States in a number of universites and, in 1967, was visiting professor at Northwestern University.*

His work has received the attention of many critics, including Foucault, Barthes, Aragon, and Sollers. In 1988 Jacqueline Risset published her Marcelin Pleynet, poète d'aujourd'hui *in the Seghers collection.*

Serge Gavronsky is Professor of French at Barnard College, Columbia University, and has translated from the French extensively. He is also a poet and a literary critic.

Pablo Picasso
The Dream and Lie of General Franco
Translated from the Spanish by Jerome Rothenberg

owl fandango escabeehe swords of octopus of evil omen furry dishrag
scalps afoot in middle of the skillet bare balls popped into a cone
of codfish sherbert fried in scabies of his oxen heart—mouth full
of marmalade of bedbugs of his words—silver bells & cockle shells
& guts braided in a row—a pinky in erection not a grape & not a
fig—commedia dell'arte of bad weaving & smudged clouds—cos-
metics of a garbarge truck—the rape of las meninas cries & out-
cries—casket on shoulders crammed with sausages and mouths—
rage that contorts the drawing of a shadow that lashes teeth nailed
into sand the horse ripped open top to bottom in the sun which
reads it for the flies who tack a rocket of white lilies to the knots
spliced in the sardine heavy nets—lamp of lice where dog is & a
knot of rats & hide outs in a palace of old rags—the banners frying
in the skillet twist in black of ink sauce spilled in drops of blood
that gun him down—the street soars to the clouds its feet bound to
a sea of wax that makes its guts rot & the veil that covers it is singing
dancing mad with sorrow—a flight of fishing poles *alhigui* and
alhigui of the moving van first class interment—broken wings spin-
ning in the spider web of dry bread & clear water a paella made of
sugar & of velvet that paints a whiplash on its cheeks—the light
blocked out the eyes before the mirror that make monkeyshines
the chunk of nougat in the flames that gnaws itself the lips around
the wound—cries of children cries of women cries of birds cries of
flowers cries of wood & stone cries of bricks cries of furniture of
beds of chairs of curtains of casseroles of cats & papers cries of
smells that claw themselves of smoke that gnaws the neck of cries
that boil in cauldron & the rain of birds that floods the sea that eats
into the bone & breaks the teeth biting the cotton that the sun
wipes on its plate that bourse & bank hide in the footprint left
imbedded in the rock.

Pablo Picasso began writing poetry in 1935 and did so for most of the rest of his life.

Jerome Rothenberg is well known as a poet and performance artist. With Pierre Joris, he edited Poems for the Millennium, *the second volume of which was recently published by the University of California Press. He has translated numerous authors, including Federico García Lorca — whose* Suites *will be published by Sun & Moon next year — Vitezslav Nezval and Kurt Schwitters. He is also the editor of* Technicians of the Sacred, Revolution of the Word, *and* Shaking the Pumpkin. *Among his most recent books of poetry are* Khurbn and Other Poems *and* Gematria *(Sun & Moon Press).*

Miroslav Holub

A Not-So-Brief Reflection on an Edict

Translated from the Czech by Michael Henry Heim

NE TAK STRUČNÁ UVAHA O EDIKTU

[The Czech below represents an earlier version of the poem]

Edikt, patrně Diokleciánův,
vyvěšsen roku 201 na tržišti v Aizanoi,
v kameni stanoví

Muž od 16 do 40 let ...30 000 denárů
Zena věku téhož ...25 000 denárů
Homo ab annis LX superius et VIII inferius ...15 000 denárů
Mulier — tedy žena — aetatis " ...10 000 denárů
Kůň jezdecký ...100 000 denárů
Equus militaris primae formae ...36 000 denárů
Dromedarius optimus ...20 000 denárů
Vacca — tedy kráva — formae primae ...2 000 denárů
Capra — tedy koza — formae primae ...600 denárů

Jsou to ceny zajisté kulantní,
za vojenského koně tři holčičky do osmi let
a deset dobrých koz není nijak moc,
ostatně kdo ví, co z holčiček vyroste,

za dva muže produktivního věku
jsou dokonce tři dromedáři,
na výživu mnohem nenáročnější,
neboť v nouzi mohou pít i svou vlastní moč

a kdo by dnes nabídl takřka sedm starců
za jezdeckého koně grošáka,
ještě tak Richard III, ale
to už je taky dávno,

za zavraždění věřitele se dnes platí
míň než za Mercedes 230,

A NOT-SO-BRIEF REFLECTION ON AN EDICT

The edict, apparently by Diocletian
And posted in the year 201 in the marketplace at Aizanoi,
States in stone:

A man from sixteen to forty	…30,000 denárii
woman of the same age	…25,000 denárii
Homo ab annis LX superius et VIII inferius	…15,000 denárii
Mulier—a woman—ætatis"	…10,000 denárii
A horse bred for riding	…100,000 denárii
Equus militaris primæ formæ	…36,000 denárii
Dromedarius optimus	…20,000 denárii
Vacca—a cow—formæ primæ	… 2,000 denárii
Capra—a goat—formæ primæ	…600 denárii

Clearly fair prices these:
A military horse for three girls under eight
Plus ten good goats is not exorbitant.
Besides, who can tell how the girls will turn out,

For two men in their prime
You get three whole dromedaries,
Which are much simpler to feed:
In case of need they can drink their urine.

Who today would give nearly seven graybeards
For a single dapple-gray.
Richard III perhaps, though
That was long ago,

Today you can have a creditor slain
For less than a Mercedes 230,

za fotbalistu primae formae
řekněme libra zlata, což bylo 72 000 denárů

a to by už musel být špion, aby
za jeho hlavu daly tajné služby cenu
osmi hošíků školy základní,
či stádo frýžských krav friského plemene.
Stádo holčiček vydělá za měsíc na ulici
jen tak na dvouhrbého velblouda,
což bylo 60 000...Kdepak! Diokleciánovy ceny
byly kulatní a hlavně vůbec byly.

Je ovšem odporné prodávat otroky na trhu;
i když tu a tam země se nadýmá a po tisících rodí
bezcenné žluté, černé a bílé, krvavé hlavy,
kvašiorkorová bříška jako korálky růžence,

jenž vede k absolutnu nebeských kantýn,
jakož i ze svíjejících se sklovitých kukel
vylézají prst po prstu, se zmačkanými nehty,
jako lišejové, nevratné ruce,

a tápají po planinách, kde bezrucí
filozofové pasou vatové tampony,
kde nejde ani tak o krev,
jako o buničinu.

Ruce tápají a zatínají se
a rosolovatí v posledním tažení,
když už není ani na filozofii,
ani na císaře, ani na zmrzlinu.

Je ovšem odporné prodávat otroky na trhu,
i když vzteklý báník vyvolává své ceny
za pravotočivé metafyzické mušle,
za hadí zádumné haveloky,

And a footballer primæ formæ
Goes for, say, a pound of gold, which was 72,000 denarii,

And it would take a superspy
To be exchanged
For eight schoolboys or a herd
Of Phrygian cows of Frisian stock.

A herd of girls on the streets would take a month
To pay for a two-humped camel,
Which came to 60,000... No, Diocletian's prices
Were fair and, more important, clearly stated.

Of course selling slaves in the marketplace rankles,
Even if a country swells here and there and gives birth
By the thousands to worthless black, white, yellow
Blood-spattered heads and kwashiorkor bellies,

A rosary leading to the absolute of celestial canteens
Much as, finger by finger, nails crushed,
Disposable hands crawl like moss-covered moths
Out of vitreous, writhing chysalides

And grope across plateaus where handless
Philosophers graze cotton-wool tampons,
Where blood has less meaning
Than cellulose.

The hands grope and clench, turn
To jelly in the final moments
When nothing remains for philosophy
Or the emperor or even ice-cream.

Of course sellng slaves in the marketplace rankles,
Even if the furious poet goes hawking
His dextral metaphysical mussels,
His snake-like contemplative cloaks.

halící vlahé vulkány hlubin,
v nichž by zasla i stydká kost,
i když básník sní o samolození genitálů,
rozesetých v mlází jako vřeckaté houby.

A poezie pak připomíná
stopadesát kočičích očí
naložených v octě, aby
bylo vidět na nesmrtelnost.

Je ovšem odporné prodávat otroky na trhu,
když i spirochety dneska memorují
habeas corpus act a člověk dosahuje ke hvězdám
a černým dírám už od stádia gastruly.

Je ovšem odporné prodávat otroky na trhu:
i když hodnotu člověka nikdo nezná,
i když hodnotu toho kterého člověka,
i když hodnotu,
i když člověka…

Ach ano, Diokleciáne.
Ten edikt ještě poněkud platí,
jednak poněkud v praxi,
jednak poněkud v tak zvané duši.

Shrouding the moist volcanos of the depths
Large enough for even a pubis,
Even if the poet dreams of self-generating genitals
Dotting the underbrush like morel mushrooms.

And what poetry recalls then
Is a hundred and fifty cat's-eyes
Cured in vinegar to see
The way to immortality.

Of course weighing people in the marketplace rankles,
Even if Dante's *Inferno* is measured in degrees Celsius
And Sisyphus' labors in kilojoules
And Diocletian's pressure on the base in newtons.

And we each of us write
Our small daily edicts
In the marketplace of night,
In our morning home.

In the permanent cave
Of our genome.

Born in Plzeň, Czechoslavkia, in 1923, Miroslav Holub received an N.D. from the Charles University School of Medicine in Prague and a Ph.D. in immunology from the Institute of Microbiology of the Czechoslovak Academy of Sciences.

Holub began writing in the late 1950s. His first volume of verse, Denní služba *(Day Duty) appeared in 1958. Over the next decade he published six more collections of poetry, including* Kam teče krev *(Where Blood Flows) in 1963 and* Tak zvané srdce *(The So-Called Heart) in 1963. In the last few years, he has begun to publish again at home. He has had numerous English-language translations, including* Selected Poems *(London: Penguin, 1967);* Notes of a Clay Pigeon *(London: Secker and Warburg, 1977);* Sagittal Section *(Oberlin, Ohio: Oberlin College Press, 1980);* On the Contrary

(Newcastle upon Tyne: Bloodaxe, 1984); and Interferon: or, On the The-
atre *(Oberlin, Ohio: Oberlin College Press, 1982).*

*Through combining a language of extreme nuance with a highly lyric
sensibility, Holub has eschewed romanticism and chosen a diction of scien-
tific precision and intricacy.*

*Michael Henry Heim is a professor in the Slavic Languages Department at
the University of California, Los Angeles and is a noted translator from the
Czech and other languages.*

)

Ștefan Augustin Doinaș

Two Poems

*Translated from the Romanian by Julian Semilian
and Sanda Agalidi*

SOMNAMBULUL

Tu—care ştii prea bine ce precar e
umbletul meu aici pe-acoperiş,
pe-aceste ţigle verzi şi-alunecoase,
pândit în jur de golul fără fund
(spion paraşutat de noapte-n ţara
în care-o pasăre e împărat):
tu—care ştii ce fire-adânci mă leagă
de-ai mei, de cei ce mă respiră-n somn
ca pe aroma unui mări pierdute
(un timp sunt încă nenăscut, apoi
de-a pururi am să fiu cu el alături);
tu— care ştii cât e de-ngustă puntea
între prăpastia fără-nceputuri
şi cealaltă care n-are capăt
(o, luna miorlăind îngroaşă noaptea
subtilul fir de-argint pe care calc);
tu încă nu mă vrei; mă laşi să umblu
cu mâinile întinse pipăind
ceva ce poate am purtat odată
pe dinăuntru—poate-un fruct în pârgă
(cât timp nu-i spui pe nume, el se coace
hrănindu-se din îndoiala mea).
Ci eu aud sub limba ta, ca-n trunchiul
scobit al unui fag o veveriţă
cum se agită albul strigăt care,
sărind asupra mea, mă va trezi.

THE SLEEPWALKER

You—who know too well how treacherous is
my walking here on the roof,
on these green and slippery tiles
stalked all around by the bottomless void
(spy parachuted by night in a land
where the emperor is a bird):
you who know what deep strings attach me
to my own, those who breathe me in their sleep
like the aroma of a lost sea.
(a while I am yet unborn,and then
I will always be with him);
You who know how narrow the plank is
between the beginningless abyss
and the other which is endless.
(o how the moon shriek fattens at night
the subtle strand of silver I tread)
you don't want me yet; you let me walk
with arms forward groping
for something I think I once toted
on the inside—maybe some fruit that wasn't ripe yet
(as long as you don't say the name, it ripens
feeding on my riddles)
Still, I hear under your tongue, like in the hollowed trunk
of a beech tree a squirrel,
how the white shout fidgets, the shout
which, leaping upon me, will wake me up.

Aici se cuvenea să fie gard:
leproşi cu frunţi muşcate, în grădină,
de pliscul unor păsări care ard;
dincolo—vinovaţii fără vină.

Dar e mai bine-aşa: astîimpărat
de vraiştea fiinţei, fiecare
uzurpă stele crude—împărat
peste tărîmul fără vindecare...

Here you should have had a fence:
lepers with foreheads bitten, in the garden,
by the beak of birds on fire;
Over there—the guilty without guilt.

Still, it's better like this: soothed
by the turmoil, each
stabs at the raw stars—emperor
over a land without ease.

One the most outstanding of contemporary Romanian poets Ştefan Augustin Doinaş is a member of the Romanian Academy and Doctor Honoris Causa of the Luican Blaga University in Sibiu. He is also a playwright, essayist, and translator.

He was born on April 26, 1922 in the small town of Caporal Alexa in the Arad country. Among his many works of poetry are The Man with the Campasses *(1966),* Laokoon's Kin *(1967),* Hypostases *(1968),* The Discreet Season *(1975),* Hesperia *(1980),* Hawk Hunt *(1985);* The Inside of a Poem *(1990),* The Laments *(1994), and* The Adventures of Proteus *(1995). His five volumes of literary criticism and essays include* Diogenes's Lamp *(1968),* Orpheus and the Temptation of the Real *(1974),* The Reading of Poetry *(1980), and* The Masks of Poetic Truth *(1992). Among the many figures he has translated into Romanian are Dante, Goethe, Hölderlin, Mallarmé, Valéry, Papini, and Nietzsche.*

In the wake of the 1956 Hungarian uprising, Doinaş was arrested as a "sympathizer," and was imprisoned for one year, along with many poets and intellectuals. Since that time, he has received most of the major Romanian writers' awards, as well as the prestigious Goethe Medal (in 1982) and the European Literature Award (in 1990).

Poet Julian Semilian was born in Romania, and works as a film editor in Los Angeles.

Sanda Agalidi is a professor of art history at the California Institute of the Arts near Los Angeles. Together the two are working on a volume of contemporary Romanian poetry, which will be published by Sun & Moon Press.

Gilbert Sorrentino
A Connoisseur's Guide to the Bay Area

> *When news reached San Francisco that on January 24,*
> *1848, James W. Marshall had picked up a gold nugget*
> *on the South Fork of the American River, its first effect*
> *was to depopulate the town.*
> *—The WPA Guide to California* (1939)

1   *Sleep, the Sun Is Shining*

A lavender sky slathered above
the unseen ocean. Violet.   Purple.
It makes us wish to be home.
Where oceans are actual oceans.

What am I doing here? is what
I am doing here. Hello, they say,
see you soon: or drop by! They
don't know how to speak

yet often they speak of dining.
Sometimes of opera or theatre and always
of the city, ah, the "City."
Soft, they are soft they are mush

in the moxie, watery.   They
confide in cars, conspire, don't like
other cars that take up *their* room.
They also like big trees. And ducks.

Oh here they come! Right back where
they started from. Back where the
brown grass blazes and the
mud slides slide golden brown.

They often walk out of the fog
and the "low clouds along
the coast" right into some
wine extravaganza.

The sun whacks them
in the head their brains boil
but they mumble lexus and
mercedes as they jog away,

smokeless and sweet. But there
are many more to come, on bikes
and wrapped in spandex breathing in
that invisible and absolutely

fine and okay carbon monoxide
lead and arsenic and blank death,
what they can't see may be
an orange or a rugged muffin!

Are they right or are they
right? Are they okay? Are they
reasonable? Are they thinking of
the stinking saintly homeless? Well!

They don't like you they come
shoot you, in Vietnamese Spanish
or English with a Giants cap.
Firestorms raze the patios.

Have a piece of shark! Want
to hold my pistol?
Another chump gets washed into
the sea off picturesque

Point Santa Nada. Then
they all hop in the car
and speed through the shit
brown tinder hills.

To buy a pot a glass of
Cabernet or Zinfandel or
a cuppa latte. What a life!
Back in the white Sentrolla

they're home in time to see
the books fall down again
from another quake. There goes
Wallace Stegner on the floor.

Those were the days at Berkeley
remember the days at Stanford
remember the acid poster art
and remember the sunny crowds!

Remember how they all stopped
the war, that's right, just sat
all down in the fucking nude
and that was it for death, man.

Jesus do you recall when
things really meant things, like
the whole red span of the Golden Gate
was crazy? Do you recall

the days when the arts
were, well, the peoples' arts! The
poems and the poems and the poems
and the bodhisattva bus!

When every washed up bust out
sweetheart of a swell guy said
that it was all going to be like
authentically weird forever? Yes suh.

Sure, the quality of life that is
the style of life that is to say
the life style is such that, well.
You see the gardens? The frazzled sun?

Certainly you do! Here is that
certain something how to say
a kind of, ah, "quality." Fog.
Couple of lost decrepit whales.

Down we go one cute street. Up we go.
Another. Spanish is fine.
In its own place. Will you
just look at these people right

on the streets. Seems that they're
looking for some kind of work? But
the crack of the bat the white whiz
of the ball! The shirts in the crowd.

And not just any crowd. This is
the quality crowd of stunned lawns and
the right sort of you know.
Don't cotton much to actual people.

Books say everybody can live forever
under depressing aerobic arms, there
you go. No reason why anyone
should actually die, come on!

Trees, ceaselessly
grey-green trees, sprayers
thunk expensively. The bicycles.
Glinting in baleful sunlight.

From one street to the other
all these items laugh that life
responds gratefully to low fat
and to high fiber and to running

here. And there. Mostly away away!
Complete with cellular plastic and
bad chanteuses vapid lyrics that
go vapid lyrics that go vapid

lyrics that go vapid lyrics that go
on. They are running faster into
the mist the low clouds the
fog the smog to life without end!

In the pollinated air
they walk backward as they
smile: Hello! You can't
beat this weather this weather.

They relentlessly put space
between their smiles and you
so that you seem to be in
weird pursuit importunate.

You soon understand that
they pretend this human trait
and that one. They are not
reasonable comatose.

They would by God love you
over for a drink and to see
the blown wisteria and the
mesquite charcoal! Spring is here.

If you should miraculously
arrive for Christ's sake don't
knock don't! They'll open
the door amazed and quite alarmed.

If you like you can sit out
in the blue fumes. You can
have a whole oat bran wheat
muffin and an immaculate water.

You can avoid satanic cigarettes
while you rev up the new
Aventra that will soon run on
that same great water.

Certainly! This is what
I can do too. Instead of
what? Instead of
what? (Sunglasses time.)

It never rains a cat or
dog that it don't grow a tree!
Right. Trees are mostly OK.
They're opening a new live oak

factory here soon. Not near
the half-million-dollar boxes
where the people who value "open"
space sort of live. Of course.

The stars are being pitched into
the imported sparkling water
from Gstaad and the waves
are avocado green

to set off the fresh-ground
coffee with the snappy monicker:
Arab indigo triple mint vanilla.
Open up that Golden Gate!

The last golden straw might
well be the hot dogs in
foil the buns in plastic wrap
out at the Old Ball Game.

Pathetic shiny packs to eat
in the parking-lot mud. Sh.
Sit, pal, the stars hover
fetchingly each night. The

stars are trig. And right.
Deep in the heart of which-its
the dock of yachtses. The dark
of vast machines always alert.

Friends, one of the facts
oft whispered to the Marines
is that a city is only a city but
San Francisco is something else.

Where else can you find
certain things? And hear the high
fine sound of first-class?
Not one of you can deny

if I'm not mistaken that when
you take this street it leads you
to the gala! And that one to
the weekend celebration, with candles.

Plenty of them! To divers arias
loads of authentic art and cuisine
this home of amazing says Hi!
Welcomes you and welcomes you

again. And yet again. When in
the slightest doubt, shoot over
sundry bridges while the bay
doth glint. Or smiling jump off same.

Born in Brooklyn, New York in 1929, Gilbert Sorrentino was the editor of the magazine Neon *in the 1950s, and in the early 1960s served as one of the editors of* Kulchur. *From 1965 to 1970 he worked as an editor for Grove Press. For the last many years he has been a Professor of English at Stanford University.*

His writing career began in 1960 with the publication of The Darkness Surrounds Us, *and over the next three decades he produced some 25 books of fiction, poetry, and criticism. Among these books are* The Sky Changes

(1966), The Perfect Fiction (1968), Imaginative Qualities of Actual Things (1971), Splendide-Hotel (1973), White Sail (1977), *and* The Orangery (1978), *which was recently reprinted by Sun & Moon Press. With the publication of* Mulligan Stew *in 1979, Sorrentino achieved international recognition, and his next fiction,* Aberration of Starlight, *extended his international audience. In 1981 Black Sparrow Press published his* Selected Poems: 1958-1980. *Among his works of the 1980s and 1990s are* Crystal Vision (1981), Blue Pastoral (1983), Something Said: Essays (1984), Odd Number (1985), Rose Theatre (1987), Under the Shadow (1991), *and* Red the Fiend (1995). *Sun & Moon Press will publish his newest fiction,* Gold Fools, *in 1999.*

Andrea Zanzotto

(PERCHÉ)   (CRESCA)

Translated from the Italian by Paul Vangelisti

(PERCHÉ)   (CRESCA)

Perché cresca l'oscuro
perché sia giusto l'oscuro
perché, ad uno ad uno, degli alberi
e dei rameggiare e fogliare di scuro
venga più scuro —
perché tutto di noi venga a scuro figliare
così che dare ed avere più scuro
albero ad uniche radici si renda — sorgi
        nella morsura scuro — tra gli alberi — sorgi
dal non arborescente per troppa fittezza
notturno incombere, fumo d'incombere:
vieni, chine già salite su chine, l'oscuro,
vieni, fronde cadute salite su fronde, l'oscuro,
succhiaci assai nel bene oscuro nel cedere oscuro,
per rifarti nel gioco istante ad istante
di fogliame oscuro in oscuro figliame
Cresci improvviso tu: l'oscuro gli oscuri:
e non ci sia d'altro che bocca
accidentata peggio meglio che voglia di consustanziazione
voglia di salvazione — bocca a bocca — d'oscuro
Lingua saggi aggredisca s'invischi in oscuro
noi e noi lingue-oscuro
Perché cresca, perché s'avveri senza avventarsi
ma placandosi nell'avverarsi, l'oscuro,
Ogni no di alberi   no di sentieri
no del torto tubero no delle nocche
no di curve di scivolii lesti d'erbe
Perché cresca e si riabbia, si distolga in spazi
in strazi in paci in armi tese all'oscuro —
mano intesa all'oscuro, mano alla bella oscura,
dita di mano mai stanche
di pervincolarsi intingersi addirsi all'oscuro
Lingue sempre al troppo, al dolcissimo soverchio

(THAT)   (IT GROW)

That the dark grow
that the dark be just
that, one by one, from the trees
and branching out and the darkly foliating
it become darker —
that all there be of us become dark foaling
so that giving and having darker
tree yield to its only roots — rise
        darkly in the etching — among the trees — rise
from the non-arborescent for too much thickness
nocturnal overhanging, overhanging smoke:
come, slopes already gone up slopes, the dark
come, fallen boughs already gone up boughs, the dark,
suck us much in dark goodness in dark surrendering,
to remake yourself in the play moment to moment
of dark foliage in foaling darkly
You grow suddenly: dark darknesses:
and there be nothing other than mouth
paralyzed worse better than craving for consubstantiation
craving for salvation — mouth to mouth — darkly
Tongue attack essays trap itself in dark
us and us tongues-dark
That it grow, that it come to pass without hurry
but calming in the coming to pass, the dark,
Every no of trees   no of paths
no of the twisted tuber no of the knuckles
no of curves of quick slips on grass
That it grow and anger, remove itself to spaces
torments treaties weapons tense against the dark —
hand aimed at the dark, hand to the dark beauty,
fingers of a hand never tired
of being bound dipped suited to the dark —
Tongues always too much, to sweetest excess

d'oscuro agglutinate, due che bolle di due —
clamore, alberi, intorno all'oscuro
clamore susù fino a disdirsi in oscuro
fino al pacifico, gridato innesto, nel te, nell'io, nell'oscuro
Innesto e ritorni di favore, fòmite oscuro
oh tu, di oscuro in oscuro innestato, tu
protratta detratta di foglia in foglia/oscuro,
di felce in felce lodata nel grezzo nel rifinito d'oscuro
Ma vedi e non puoi vedere quanto è d'oscuro qui dentro
hai bevuto lingua e molto più e sentieri e muschi intrusi
ma ti assicuri ti accingi ti disaccorgi
ti stratifichi, lene, benedetta, all'oscuro

Non-memoria, millenni e miglia, stivate nel fornice
sono un dito dell'oscuro, levalo dalla bocca, rendilo nocca
rovina e ripara l'oscuro, così sarà furto e futuro
Troppo dell'inguine, del ventre, di ghiande e glandole
s'inguina in oscuro, genera generi, intride glie
Precipitare fuori bacio, scoagularsi, venire a portata
d'ogni possible oscuro
Possibili alberi, alberi a se stessi oscuri
mai sazi mai di accedere a frotte
a disorientarsi a orientare, lievito intollerabile
Limo d'oscuro che dolce fòrnica pascola
nei fornici dove s'aggruma di fughe   (l'oscuro)

            E pluralità innumerabile di modalità
            dell'oscuro, secarsi in innumerevoli — non due —
                        d'oscuro sessi

Qui in feccia, all'oscuro, immanere
Là in volta, all'oscuro, esalarsi
Possibile, alberi — Possibile, oscuri, oscuro.
            Oscuro ha sé, sessuata, umiltà
                        tracotanza, pietà.

of agglutinated dark, two that boils with two —
clamor, trees, around the dark
clamor up and up to retracting in darkness
to the pacific, grafted shouting, in the you, in the I, in the dark
Grafted and recurrence of favor, dark source
oh you, grafted from dark to dark, you
protracted subtracted from leaf into leaf/dark,
from fern to fern praised in the raw in the worn out with dark
But you see and cannot see how much of the dark is in here
you have drunk tongue and much more and paths and intrusive moss
but you assure yourself gird yourself become unaware
lie in layers, soft, blessed, in the dark

Non-memory, millennia and miles, stowed in the fornix
are a finger of the dark, take it out of your mouth, make it knuckle
ruin and repair the dark, so will it be fraud and future
Too much groin, belly, acorns and glands
groins itself in the dark, generates genders, soaks neuroglia
Precipitating out of a kiss, uncoagulating yourself, coming into range
of every possible darkness
Possible trees, trees dark to themselves
never sated never of entering in crowds
to being disoriented oriented, intolerable yeast
slush of dark that sweetly fornicates grazes
in the fornices where it bunches up with flight   (the dark)

> And innumerable plurality of modality
> of the dark, drying up in numberless—not two —
> sexes of dark

Here in the dregs, in the dark, immanent
There in the vault, in the dark, expiring yourself
Possible, trees—Possible, darknesses, dark.
> Dark has itself, sexualized, humility,
> haughtiness, pity.

Born in Pieve di Soligo on October 10, 1921, Andrea Zanzotto earned his degree in letters from the University Padua in 1942. During this same period he took part in the Resistance, spending time in France and Switzerland after the war.

One of Zanzotto's first champions was the noted Italian poet Eugenio Montale, who described Zanzotto as "the most important Italian poet born in this century."

Although Zanzotto's career, spanning five decades, is marked by dramatic stylistic turns, his major issues have remained in focus, and he has continued to write a poetry that explores self and its links with nature and culture. Zanzotto has also been influenced by major cultural thinkers of the Twentieth Century, including Martin Heidegger, Roman Jakobson and Jacques Lacan.

Among his many collections are Dietro il paesaggio *(1951),* Elegia e altri versi *(1954),* Vocativo *(1957),* IX Ecloghe *(1962),* La Beltà *(1968),* Pasque *(1973),* Idioma *(1968),* Filò per il Casanova di Fellni *(1988), and* Meteo *(1996). The selection here is from his book,* Il Galateoin Bosco *(1978).*

Friederike Mayröcker

Three Poems

*Translated from the German by Rosmarie Waldrop
and Harriett Watts*

© Heidi Heide

*Winner of the 1997 International Prize of
the America Awards, Friederike
Mayröcker was born in Vienna in 1924.
She attended business school before be-
ing drafted, from 1942 to 1945, into the
Luftwaffe. At the same time, she trained
as a school teacher, and after the war she
taught school until 1969, when she de-
voted full time to her poetry.*

*Mayröcker has been awarded several
other major literary prizes, including the
Theodor Körner Prize (1963), the Georg Trakl
Prize for poetry (1977), and the Great Austrian State Prize (1982).*

Books in German

Larifari (Wein: Bergland Verlag, 1956); *metaphorisch* (Stuttgart, Max Bense
und Elisabeth Walther, 1965); *texte* (Innsbruck: allerheiligenresse, 1966);
Tod durch Musen (Reinbek: Rowohlt, 1966); *Sägespäne für mein Herzbluten*
(Berlin: Rainer-Verlag, 1967); *Minimonsters Traumlexikon* (Reinbek:
Rowohlt, 1968); *Fantom Fan* (Reinbek: Rowohlt, 1971); *Fünf Mann
Menschen, Hörspiele* (Neuwied: Luchterhand Verlag, 1972); *Arie auf
tönernen Füszen, Metaphysisches Theater* (Neuwied: Luchterhand, 1972);
Blaue Erleuchtungen (Düsseldorf: Verlag Eremiten Presse, 1972); *je ein
umwölkter gipfel* (Neuwied: Luchterhand, 1973); *in langsamen Blitzen*
(Düsseldorf: Verlag Eremiten Presse, 1974); *Augen wie Schaljapin bevor er
starb, Kurzprosa* (Dornbirn: Vorarlberger Verlagsanstalt, 1974); *Das Licht
in der Landschaft, Prosa* (Frankfurt: Suhrkamp Verlag, 1975); *schriftungen:
oder gerùchte aus dem jenseits, Pros* (Pfaffenweiler: Verlag Pfaffenweiler,
1975); *Drei Hörspiele* (Wein: Sessler Verlag, 1975); *Fast ein Frùhling des
Markus M* (Frankfurt: Suhrkamp Verlag, 1976); *rot ist unten, Prosa,*

Gedichte, Hörspiele (Wein: Verlag Jugend und Volk, 1977); *heisze hunde, Prosa* (Pfaffenweiler: Verlag Pfaffenweiler Presse, 1977); *Heiligenanstalt* (Frankfurt: Suhrkamp Verlag, 1978); *lütt'kock, ein Gedicth in 6 Phasen* (Wein: herbstpresse, 1978); *Tochter der Bahn, Prosa* (Düsseldorf: Verlag Eremited Presse, 1979); *Ausgewählte Gedichte 1944-1978)* (Frankfurt: Suhrkamp Verlag, 1979); *Ein Lesebuch, Gedichte, Prosa, Hörspiele* (Frankfurt: Suhrkamp Verlag, 1979); *Schwarmgesang, Hörspiele* (Berlin: Rainer-Verlag, 1979); *Die Abschiede, Prosa* (Frankfurt: Suhrkamp Verlag, 1980); *schwarze Romanzen* (Pfaffenweiler: Pfaffenweiler Presse, 1981); *Treppen, Prosa* (St. Pölten: Verlag Niederösterreichisches Pressehaus, 1981); *Bocca della Verita, Hörspiel* (Wein: ORF, 1981); *ich, der Rabe und der Mond* (Graz: Verlag Maximilian Droschl, 1981); *Gute Nacht, guten Morgen, Gedichte 1978-1981* (Frankfurt: Suhrkamp Verlag, 1982); *Magische Blätter, Prosa* (Frankfurt: Suhrkamp Verlag, 1983); *im Nervensaal, Prosa* (Wein: herstpresse, 1983); *Das Anheben der Arme bei Feuersglud, Gedichte, Prosa* (Stuttgart: Reclams Universalbibliothek, 1984); *Reise durch de Nacht, Prosa* (Frankfurt: Suhrkamp Verlag, 1984); *Kockodan Samota (meerkatze Einsamkeit, Gedichte* (Prag: Odeon Verlag, 1984); *Rosengarten, Prosa* (Pfaffenweiler: Verlag Pfaffwnweiler Presse, 1985); *Configurationen, Prosa zu Bildern von Hubert Aratym* (wein: Verlag sonderzahl, 1985); *Das Herzzereiszende der Dinge, Prosa* (Frankfurt: Suhrkamp Verlap, 1990); *Das Jahr Schnee, Gedichte, Prosa, Hörspiele* (Wein: Verlag Volk un Welt/Berlin DDR, 1985); *Winterglück, Gedichte 1982-1985)* (Frankfurt: Suhrkamp Verlag, 1986); *der Donner des Stillhaltens, Prosa* (Verlag Maximilian droschl, 1986); *Magische Blätter II, Prosa* (Frankfurt: Suhrkamp Verlag, 1987); *mein Herz mein Zimmer mein Name, Prosa* (Frankfurt: Suhrkamp Verlag, 1988); *Dekomposition* (Frankfurt: Edition Irmgard Flemming, 1989); *Umbra, der Schatten, Prosa zu Arbeiten von Linde Waber* (Wein: Hora Verlag, 1989); *Jericho, Gedicht in mehreren Phasen* (Wein: herstpresse, 1989); *Variantenverzeichnis, oder Abendempfindung an Laura, Prosa* (Bonn: Edition Octopus Okeanos Presse, 1989); *Gesammelte Prose 1949-1975)* (Frankfurt: Suhrkamp Verlag, 1989); *aus einem Stein entsprungen* (St. Gallen: erker verlag, 1989); *Entfachung, Gedicht in mehreren Phasen* (Wein: Edition mohs, 1990); *empfindliche Träume* (Wein: herstpresse, 1990); *Magische Blätter III, Prosa* (Frankfurt: Suhrkamp Verlag, 1991); *Stilleben, Prosa* (Frankfurt: Suhrkamp Verlag, 1991); *das besessene Alter, Neue Gedichte* (Frankfurt: Suhrkamp Verlag, 1992); *Phobie der Wäsche* (Köln: edition fundamental, 1992); *LECTION* (Frankfurt: Suhrkamp Verlag, 1994); *Magische Blätter IV* (Frankfurt: Suhrkamp Verlag, 1995); *Notizen auf einem Kamel, Gedichte 1991-1996)* (Frankfurt: Suhrkamp Verlag, 1996).

English Language Editions

Night Train, trans. by Beth Bjorklund (Riverside, California: Ariadne Press, 1992); *Heiligenanstalt*, trans. by Rosmarie Waldrop (Providence: Burning Deck Press, 1994); *with each clouded peak*, trans. by Rosmarie Waldrop and Harriett Watts (Los Angeles: Sun & Moon Press, 1998).

DIE VOGEL KUTSCHE

für Christa Kühnhold

waren es Hühner Kinder Bachstelzen Buch-
staben welche am Weiher und in den Wiesen :
Wolken üppigen Wolken und Wiesen : wogend
und in welchen man sah 3 Gestalten mit strohgelben
van-Gogh-Hüten…diese Unschuld diese Umschweife
zum See und der knisternde Blech Kübel bei verhangenem
Wetter das waren Granatäpfel nämlich Tropfen aus
einem Gewitter Himmel : aus einer Dachtraufe ein
Knattern und Nadel Instrument unerkläliches
Wetter Instrument, usw., die Lauch Gewächse und
Paraplues im Wald über den Geraniengärten wenn
man sie dem Regen überläszt dann fangen sie an
dann bluten sie nämlich der weisze Schirm wie
er in der Blumen Erde gesteckt hat : Firn- oder
Firnis Schnee auf dem Nacken des Gebirges, an
der Kreide Tafel der griechischen Gaststätte
gegen das Tor gelehnt, stand, an der Spitze
der Speisenfolge ein Gericht wie GOTTES LAMM / DAS
LAMM GOTTES, im Kostüm des Regens und Herolds :
1 schwarzes Ästchen war so gebeugt und geknickt
nämlich vom Baum gebrochen dasz es die
Initiale des Dichters beschrieb.

THE BIRD COACH

for Christa Kühnhold

was it chickens children lapwings letterings
that along the pond and in the fields :
clouds lush clouds and fields : rippling
and where you saw 3 figures with straw yellow
van-Gogh-hats…this innocence this indirection
toward the lake and the clattering tin bucket under overcast
weather it was pomegranates i.e. drops out of
a stormy sky : from the eaves a
rattling and for needle instrument inexplicable
weather instrument, etc., the leek plants and
parapluies in the woods above the geranium gardens when
you leave them in the rain they start
they bleed i.e. a white umbrella as if
stuck in the flowered ground : firn or
glacier snow on the nape of the mountains,
chalked on the blackboard by the door
of the Greek restaurant, at the top
of the menu a dish like GOD'S LAMB / LAMB
OF GOD, in a costume of rain and herolds :
1 black twig was so bent and twisted
i.e. broke off the tree that it
formed the poet's initial.

RW

NARRATION OF A NARRATION
from *with each clouded peak*

red, he said, red and as hard as chalk.

chalk is not hard, she said.

red, he said, and as hard as chalk, and producible from everything, he said.

from everyone, she said, by everyone producible, poetry must be producible by everyone.

from everything, he said.

revolution poetry, she said.

no, he said, no.

reality based on values, she said, contemplation.

new contemplation perhaps, he said.

a hand, he said, with a baker's tong reaching from the shop into a chock-full confectionary window, removing a segment from an already cut pie, and you in front of the window, he said.

a comparison, she said, questioningly.

intellectual compulsion toward truth, he said, intentions under strain .

like pallas athene sprung fully equipped from the head of zeus, she said questioningly.

and before the shop door a mat for the dog, he said.

a bit higher a hook to hang the leash, he said, above that an enameled sign WE CANNOT ENTER and beneath it the head of a dog, he said.

you must break out, she said, *out of reality*, but break it down with you, down into the abyss as you fall.

and how did that become you, he said.

from next door, she said, i heard in the morning silence the curtains being drawn back from the windows.

some localities, he said, leave me with pleasant, others with unpleasant feelings and thoughts, he said.

paths, streets, entranceways, vistas, squares, lawns, passages, buildings, wall angles, gardens, he said, without my knowing why.

such reflections are not new to me, she said.

but what have i done wrong, why has it all gone wrong, i did all that i could to make it work.

we know much too little of each other, he said.

and then, she said, i tried out my left eye to see how it functioned. meanwhile we were walking down a side street that ran along the highway, a short stretch always back and forth as if we were waiting for someone who at any moment should come out of the house, standing without neighborhood here at the wayside, and i stared a long time into the lemon-yellow sky.

in a cold bedroom, he said, when i climb into a cold bed, slip undressed under the white wool blanket, i can tell, he said, how my bed gradually grows warm with the warmth of my body.

with the person i was at ten, he said, i have nothing more in common.

HW

the power plant glittering, he said, quite contrary to.
we walked through an arbor, the bushes trimmed.
a few old rosehips among the branches, overhanging the garden edge.
it was the shape of africa, he said, the birthmark on her forehead.
had faded with the years.
we continued on our way, he said, tottering and uncertain.
we walked through the arbor, the convent bell began to ring.
she wanted to appear modest, he said.
she was definitely downbeat in almost all respects, he said.
she may be remembered now, he said.
shrub leaf, clover, a certain reversal, he said, a figure of art.
in leaden shoes up endless stairs, he said, had to take my overcoat off while climbing, stuffed it into a big bag.
she may be remembered now, he said.
we remember having remembered.
the convent bell began to ring.
shrub leaf, clover, he said, you who stop here.
how things move into position against us, he said.
even those we've mostly done well by.
had been the shape of africa and faded with the years.
the creature exposed, he said.
free yourself, come free, he said, of this entanglement.
how, he said, the days unwind.
entry way, power plant.
he felt he could never have put out this fire, he said, a fiery mark fading on her forehead.
hissed through his teeth always the same swearword, and the stars, he said, already drumming on his skull.
she was taken aback, he said, when a strange woman in the subway asked if she had seen the giant rabbit leaping out of the tunnel.
fossilization, he said, gradual.

we went through the arbor when the convent bell began to ring.
we continued on our way, tottering and uncertain.

RW

*Rosmarie Waldrop is a well known poet, author of numerous books of poetry
and fiction, including* When They Have Senses, Peculiar, Streets Enough
to Welcome Snow, Shorter American Memory, A Key to the Language of
America, Nothing Has Changed, Differences for Four Hands, *and* A Form/
Of Taking/It All. *She has translated extensively from the French and Ger-
man. With Harriett Watts she co-edited and translated* The Vienna Group:
Six Major Austrian Poets (1985) *and the recently published Mayröcker work,*
with each clouded peak.

Elisabeth Borchers

from *Von der Grammatik des heutigen Tages*

Translated from the German by Peggy Miller

Jüngling. 18. Jahrhundert.
Alabastern, ein Holzkleid darüber.
Feines abblätterndes Gold. Lotrecht
fallende Arme und Hände. Sehr schlank.
In vollkommenem Stillstand. Bis zur Schulter
reichend. Die Bedeckung des Kopfes perlmuttverziert.
Objekt, Kunstobjekt, eine Art Wiedergeburt.
Schlaflos, resistent gegen Mondschein.
Und lächelnd, mit der dem Wuchs
des erleuchtenden Baumes entsprechenden
Vollendung.

Nur keine Rührung. Es könnte den Satzbau
stören.

Boy. 18th century.
Alabaster, overlaid in wood.
Fine goldleaf peeling. Arms and hands
hanging straight down. Very slender.
Absolutely still. Adorned up to
the shoulder. The headdress decorated with mother of pearl.
Object, art object, a kind of rebirth.
Sleepless, resistant to moonlight.
And smiling, with a perfection
reflecting the breadth of the glowing
branches.

But no emotion. It might disturb
the sentence structure.

DAS GEDICHT ALS KARAWANSEREI
ERRICHTET ZUR UNTERBRINGUNG EINER GESCHENK-KARAWANE
VORAUSGESCHICKT EINEM BALDIGEN WIEDERSEHEN ZUR
ERHÖHUNG UND BESCHWICHTIGUNG HERRSCHENDER FREUDEN

Hier abgestiegen zur Ausruh von Plage und Mühsal
im Verlauf einer langen Reise über hohen Berg, durch tiefes
Tal, durch Unbill, Wind und Meer

und angesichts der gröblich sich äussernden Ungeduld
vor allem der koketten Spitzohräffchen und gewöhnlichen
Königstiger, der konjugierten Karauschen und Karbatschen,
eines nicht dazu gehörenden Lichtjahres, eines Knöchelchens
vom Spatz, der das Schuhband des heiligen Franziskus löste,
des blauen Firnis, einer Zisterne mit dem Ausmass der guten
Hoffnung, jenes prächtig gewandeten Mohrenknaben, der
eine silberne Busine bläst, der Postmoderne in Form einer
gläsernen Hutschachtel, eines gerüttelt Masses Armerseelen
zum Zweck der Wiedergewinnung und Aberhunderter
anderer Artikel aus der derzeitigen Geschenkindustrie. Nicht
zu vergessen die zarte Ungeduld der nach Art des Schnees
in sich ruhenden Flocke vom Pelz der Gräfin Walewska

was ausserordentlich gut zu verstehen ist in dieser
Wüstenei ohne Schirm und Schutz vor Sengen und Plündern,
Frieren, Hungern und Dürsten und in der Befürchtung einer
nie endenden Reise und schwindender Freuden.

THE POEM AS CARAVANSARY
ERECTED TO ACCOMMODATE A CARAVAN OF SOUVENIRS
ANTICIPATING AN EARLY GATHERING
FOR THE PROMOTION AND APPEASEMENT OF PREVAILING PLEASURES.

    Here disembarked to rest from torment and drudgery
in the course of a long journey over high mountain, through
deep valley, through hardship, wind and sea.

    and in the face of crudely apparent impatience, especially
on the part of the coquettish little monkeys and the usual Bengal
tiger, of the conjugated crucian carp and hunting crop, of a
light year that doesn't belong here, of a little bone from the
sparrow that loosened the shoelace of St. Francis, of the blue
varnish, of a cistern with the magnitude of good hope, that
splendidly clad Moorish lad blowing a silver horn, of the
Postmodern in the form of a glass hatbox, of a struggling crowd
of wretched souls trying to redeem themselves, and several
hundred other trinkets of the current gift market. Not to forget
the delicate impatience of the flock that settles like snowflakes on
the fur coat of the Countess Walewska.

    which is extraordinarily easy to understand in this
wasteland without protection or defense against fire and pillage,
freezing cold, hunger and thirst and in the fearful anticipation
of a never ending journey and vanishing happiness.

TÜBINGEN

Einmal stand ich dort unten
Hoch oben der Turm
Und legte die Hände
Flach aufs Gestein.

Erzähl, was du weisst
Jetzt kannst du's doch sagen
Selig treibst du im Frühlicht
Wenn's dunkelt bei mir.

Sag mir keiner, du wärst schon entrückt
Hinaus aus den Höhen in höhere noch
Mit hellem Gefieder
Ich hör den Nordost.

Er ist's, der die Bäume zusammentreibt
Zu Wäldern, die Hänge der Berge hinauf
Bishin wo die Kälte beginnt
Ja, er.

Und wenn die Vögel schwärmen
Rafft er sie dahin, jagt sie gen Süden
Wie damals die Schiffe.

Doch nicht auf der schönen Garonne
Das weiss ich gewiss
Unter den Stürmen
war er ihm der liebste.

Once I stood down there
The tower high above me
And laid my hands
Flat on the stone.

Tell what you know—
Now you can say it
Blessed you move in the morning light
When it is dark for me.

Let no one say you were already carried off
Out of the heights, and up higher still
With bright plumage—
I hear the northeast.

It is he who herds the trees together
Into forests up the slopes of mountains
As high as where the cold begins
Yes, he.

And when the birds swarm
He sweeps them away, drives them south
As once the ships.

But not toward the beautiful Garonne
That I know for certain
Among the storms
that one was his favorite.

Und ich höre vom Mord
Die Tat, die die Liebe begeht
Fast hätt ich das Zeichen
vergessen.

Nichtsahnend gehst du darauf zu
Als wäre das Dunkel erleuchtet.

And I hear of murder
The act that love commits
I had nearly forgotten
that sign.

You approach it unsuspecting
As if the darkness were illuminated.

Elisabeth Borchers was born in 1926 in Hamburg, Germany. She is a lektor for the Suhrkamp publishers in Frankfurt-am-Main.

Borchers worked as an interpreter in the early postwar years in Germany, and later as a reader for publishing houses. Borchers' own poetry has appeared since 1960, when she published in the Frankfurter Allgemeine Zeitung. *The poems, "eia wasser regnet schlaf," raised a legendary storm of letters to the editor, both pro and con, because of its dark, suggestively gruesome message of what one can really do with a drunken sailor.*

Today she is highly admired in Germany as the author of five books of poetry, including Wer Lebt, *published in 1986 (winner of the Hölderlin Prize for poetry), and her most recent book,* Von der Grammatik des heutigen Tages, *published in 1992. Because of her spare uses of language, she has been dubbed the Poet of Silences.*

Borchers has also edited a noted anthology, tracing women's poetry in German through the ages, Gedichte von Hildegard von Bingen bis Ingeborg Bachmann, *and she has published numerous translations, including Marcel Proust's* Der Gleichgültige.

Peggy Miller lives in Bethesda, Maryland, where she teaches in a program affliated with American University. She is also a poet, and is finishing a manuscript titled WindSock.

Durs Grünbein

Two Poems

Translated from the German by Andrew Shields

1

Dann gingen wir schwimmen, mit den Toten auf du und du.
In eisgrauen Baggerseen Stieß der Fuß auf Gestänge
Rostiger Rohre, Maschinenteile, versenkt im Morast.

Es war dunkel dort unten. Wie offene Welsmäuler steckten
Periskope im Schlamm, Geräte tückischer Überwasserwesen,
Installiert gegen aufkommendes Leben, im Schutz der Nacht.

Vor den entzündeten Augen, wie Schlingpflanzen, lose
Trieben die Atemblasen der andern, vergebliche Wünsche,
Mit den schaukelnden Zerrbildern zurück ins Gestrüpp.

In der Haltung von Fröschen, faulenzend, zogen wir Kreise
Zwischen Ufern kaum älter als wir. In den Wasserspiegeln
Erblickten wir Sägeblätter, Kniescheiben, rotierende Schatten.

Die Hand streifte Stichlingsnester. In pfeilschnellen Trupps
Schwärmten die Zähesten aus, Pioniere im Trüben. Es galt
Keine Luft zu verlieren, verletzt unter Wasser, kein Blut.

Und jeder erzählte sie anders, Geschichten vom kalten Stern,
Von Traktoren, auf denen Skelette saßen, am Grund nachts,
Wo die Erde gefror und Liebespaare beim Baden ertranken.

Denn alles war um den einen Stachel zentriert, diesen Dorn,
Zum Aufspießen der Wolken, den uns ins Fleisch trieb
Klein, auf dem Handteller zappelnd, der erste mutierte Fisch.

TRIGEMINUS

1

Then we went swimming, on familiar terms with the dead.
In ice-gray flooded quarries, our feet ran into struts,
Rusty pipes and parts of machines, sunk in the mire.

It was dark down there. Like open catfish mouths, periscopes
Were stuck in the mud, the tools of tricky overwater creatures,
Installed against emergent life, under cover of night.

Right before our inflamed eyes, like creepers, the loose
Bubbles of breath from the others, futile wishes, drifted
With the swaying, warped reflections back into the undergrowth.

Lazing about, in the posture of frogs, we circled around
Between shores hardly older than we were. We caught a glimpse,
In the water's surface, of saw blades, kneecaps, rotating shadows.

Hands grazed the nests of sticklebacks. In lightning-swift packs,
The toughest swarmed out, pioneers in the murk, aiming
To lose no air or, injured underwater, blood.

And everyone told them differently, stories from the cold star,
Of tractors on which skeletons sat, at night on the bottom,
Where the earth was frozen and lovers drowned while swimming.

For everything was focused on a sting, this thorn
For skewering clouds, driven into our flesh by the first
Mutant fish, small and wriggling on someone's palm.

Gezeugt im verwunschenen Teil eines Landes
Mit Grenzen nach innen, war er Märchen gewöhnt,
Grausamkeit. Daß der Himmel zu hoch hing,
Grund für die Kindheitsfieber, machte ihn platt.
Später ließ es ihn kalt. Dicht wie die Fenster
Hielt er dem Außenraum stand, — ohne Ausblick.
Hinter den Hügeln, gespenstisch, zog den Schluß-
Strich kein Horizont, nur ein rostiger Sperrzaun.
Landeinwärts…gehegte Leere. Sein Biotop, früh
War ein riesiger Müllberg, von Bulldozern
Aufgeworfen, am Stadtrand. Ein Manöverfeld,
Naßkalter Sand, übersät mit Autoreifen und Schrott,
Dazu ein schillernder Teich, eine Einflugschneise,
Ein dürres Wäldchen. So bodennah sah er
Den Lerchenflug aus der Perspektive des Wurms.
Bald konnte er lesen. Und jeder Lilienthal
War ihm lieb, der bewies: Leichter als Luft zu sein,
War normal. Für die Dauer des Traums
Spann aus feinsten Düsen ihm Zeit eine Zuckerwatte
Aus Wasserstoff, unerreichbar für jeden
Abfangjäger, lautlos, ein weißes Flugobjekt.
Er war oft in Gedanken dort oben, wo ein Triebwerk
Die Wolken fräste. Daß jedes Abseits sich selbst
Das nächste war, gab seinen Blicken Halt.

Begotten in the spellbound part of a country
Whose borders were turned inwards, he was used to
Fairy tales and cruelty. The sky was too high,
Causing childhood fevers, dumbfounding him.
Later it left him cold. Sealed window-tight,
He withstood the outside world—without a view.
Behind the hills, ghostly, no horizon
Marked the end, only a rusty fence.
Inland…emptiness preserved. Still young,
His habitat was a giant mountain of garbage
Heaped up by bulldozers at the city's edge.
A field for maneuvers, cold, wet sand, strewn with tires
And junk, a shimmering pond, an airplane approach path,
An arid thicket. So close to the ground, he had
A worm's eye view of the flight of the lark.
Soon he could read. And every Lilienthal
Was dear to him who proved: to be lighter than air
Was normal. For the dream's duration,
Time spun for him a cotton candy of hydrogen
From the finest jets, beyond the reach of every
Interceptor, silent, a white flying object.
Often, he was lost in thoughts up where an engine
Milled the clouds. As every distance was closest
To itself, his gazes had something to hold.

3

Weit draußen, sobald man die Schläfen rieb, hellhörig stromernd...
Den Siedlungen fernblieb, Bahngleisen folgend und Feldern—
War man nicht fremd hier? Lag nicht gleich vor der Tür,
In den unerwiderten Rufen, im Dunkel, die Grenze
Zu einem Imperium bis zur mongolischen Steppe?
Daß man umstellt war, eingekreist von beweglichen Truppen,
Sah man erst bei Gewitter, in den Räderspuren im Wegschlamm
Oder beim Aufschein von Taschenlampen an Waldrändern abends.
Undenkbar daß ein Kind, beim Ausflug auf seinem neuen Fahrrad,
Hinter dem Drahtzaun dem fernen Kirgisen im Wachturm,
Dem sibirischen Posten nicht winken sollte, so nah.
Überall gab es Tatorte, graue Regionen. Ein kalter Atlas
Wuchs mit der Kopfhaut über Nacken und Stirn,
Mit jedem Gesichtsnerv, vom Regen erregt,
Bis man das Rauschen von innen erkannte: den Osten,
Die bleiernen Flüsse, die Ebenen, diese Erde im Dauerfrost,
Alles was groß war, verloren und weit bis nach Wladiwostok.
Jeder Schuß zog einen Strich durch den offenen Raum, eine Nacht,
An der entlang man sich trennen lernte, jedesmal etwas leichter,
Von den verwilderten Gärten, den entdeckten Verstecken im Wald.
Eines Tags, unterm Laub ein Schwelbrand (aus welcher Saga
Von Taigajägern) war da ein Ameisenbau wie ein Haufen
Knisternder Späne, in dem man brennend versank,
Noch einmal geboren, die nackten Arme verätzt.
Einer ertrank beim Schlittschuhlauf. Einer
Erbrach sich als ein andrer ein Auge verlor
Im Spiel mit gefundener Munition. Einer schrie,
Weil die Luft, wie von Sternenlicht infiziert, ihn bedrückte.
Knirschte der Schnee unterm Schritt nicht wie Insektenpanzer?
Blieb man nicht längst von zu Hause weg....in verbotenen Zonen
Unterwegs hinterm Sperrzaun, am Schlachthof, auf Aschenhalden
Mit Platzwunden täglich und wechselnden Freunden. Trennung—
Das warn die schmalen Gräben, im Auf- und Abgehn gezogen,
In kalten Händen die Zirkel, bis das Gezeter erstickte

3

Far outside, as soon as you rubbed your temples, alertly wandering…
Shunned the developments, following train tracks and fields—
Weren't you foreign here? Wasn't it right in front of
The door, in unanswered shouts, in the darkness—the border
Of an empire all the way to the steppes of Mongolia?
Only during storms did you see you were surrounded,
Encircled by mobile troops, in the wheelmarks in the muddy paths,
Or when, in the evening, the flashlights shone at the forest's edge.
Unthinkable that a child riding his brand-new bike should not
Wave to the distant Kirghiz in the watchtower,
The Siberian sentry so close behind the wire fence.
Crime scenes everywhere, gray areas. With the scalp,
An atlas grew over neck and forehead, cold,
With every facial nerve excited by rain,
Until you perceived the roaring from inside: the East,
The leaden rivers, the plains, this soil so long frozen,
Everything large, lost and distant right to Vladivostok.
Every shot made a mark across the open space, a seam
Which taught you, each time a bit more easily, how to part
With the overgrown gardens, the hideouts devised in the forest.
Once, a smoldering fire under leaves (some saga
Of taiga hunters), there was a nest of ants like a pile
Of crackling kindling you sank down into, burning,
Then born again, with naked arms singed.
One drowned while ice-skating. One
Vomited when another lost an eye
Playing with ammunition he'd found. One screamed
Because the air, as if infected by starlight, weighed down on him.
Didn't the snow crunch like insect shells at every step?
Didn't you already stay away from home…in forbidden zones
Out behind the fence, at the slaughterhouse, on ashheaps
With cuts everyday and a series of friends. Estrangement—
The narrow ditches made by walking back and forth,
The compass in cold hands, until the nagging smothered

Im Schrank zwischen alten Pullovern, Geographie-
Büchern und Lexika, einige Wetterkarten
Vor dem kurzen *Seither.*

FALTEN UND FALLEN

Leute mit besseren Nerven als jedes Tier, flüchtiger, unbewußter
Waren sie's endlich gewohnt, den Tag zu zerlegen. Die Pizza
Aus Stunden aßen sie häppchenweise, meist kühl, und nebenbei
Hörten sie plappernd CDs oder fönten das Meerschwein,
Schrieben noch Briefe und gingen am Bildschirm auf Virusjagd.
Zwischen Stapeln Papier auf dem Schreibtisch, Verträgen, Kopien,
Baute der Origami-Kranich sein Nest, eine raschelnde Falle.
Jeder Tag brachte, am Abend berechnet, ein anderes Diagramm
Fraktaler Gelassenheit, später in traumlosem Kurzschlaf gelöscht.
Sah man genauer hin, mit der aus Filmen bekannten Engelsgeduld,
Waren es Farben, verteilt wie die Hoch- und Tiefdruckzonen
Über Europas Kartentisch. Sie glichen dem Fell des Geparden
Im Säugetier-Lexikon, den Blättern fixierten Graphitstaubs
Mit Fingerabdrücken in der Kartei für Gewalttäter. Deutlich
War diese Spur von Vergessen in allen Hirnen, Faltern, Gesichtern,
Flüsternd, bis auf den Lippen das dünne Apfelhäutchen zerriß.

In the closet between the old sweaters, geography
Books and encyclopedias, a couple of weather maps
Before the brief *since-then*.

FOLDS AND TRAPS

People with better nerves than any animal, more fleeting, unconscious,
They'd finally got used to dissecting the day. They ate the pizza
Of hours bit by bit, mostly cool, and all the while listened
To CDs through their chatter, or blow-dried the guinea pig,
Even wrote letters and hunted for viruses on the screen.
Among piles of paper on the desk, the contracts and copies,
The origami crane constructed its nest, a rustling trap.
Every day offered, in evening's measure, a different diagram
Of fractual composure a short dreamless sleep later erased.
If one looked more closely, with the saintly patience known from films,
There were colors distributed like zones of high and low pressure
On Europe's map table, akin to the cheetah's fur in the book
Of mammals, the fingerprint pages of fixed graphite dust
On the cards in the violent criminal file. Clear in all
The brains, folds, and faces was this trace of forgetting, whispering
Until, on the lips, the thin membrane tore like apple skin.

*Durs Grünbein was born in Dresden in 1962. Since the break up of the
Communist bloc, he has traveled extensively in Europe, Southeast Asia,
and the United States. He has lived in Berlin since 1986. Among his books
of poetry are* Grauzone morges *(1988),* Schädelbasislektion *(1991),* Den
Teuren Toten *(1994), and* Falten und Fallen *(1996). He has received nu-
merous prizes for his books, including the most prestigious German literary
prize, the Georg Büchner Prize in 1995.*

Andrew Shields currently lives in Poitiers, France.

Ronald Johnson
from *Z's*

Stretch sublime
sunshine and me!

Rare birds we'd be
If I were free —

endless tweedledee
swallowed infinity.

pulse
prowl
psalm

curious
aloof

narrow
assassin

in quest
caress

Call me Slim
Stairway Patrol
the real McCoy
Mr. Control

Monster
sly boots
boast

arched
preamble
O salaam!

plume
coup de
grâce

precisely
beyond
reach

trace kin
Enormouse

seek race
Whiskerer

Move/
  wave
over
  evolver

  Climb
at last

 limb onto
  I'm

ping-pong
possessor
pitchdark
periphery

clout untold
flex precipice
unfold leap
in pounce Utopia:

s p r a y d
p a l e s t
c h a s e d
p e a r l s

nostril
intent
stray
flea
aft

resounding drums
I purr through room
I and I and I
renouncing doom

seeing-eye
sidekick

braid ahead
footpath

criss/cross
backtrack

pad, pad, pad

yield fourfoot

leap to a snap

furred purrer!

Born in 1935 in Ashland, Kansas, Ronald Johnson briefly attended the University of Kansas before spending two years in Korea in the United States Army. Upon his return home, he attended and graduated from Columbia University in 1960. During these New York years he became acquainted with many artists, poets, and scholars, some of whom were associated with the Black Mountain College in North Carolina. Johnson's own poetics would be highly influenced by one of the Black Mountain teachers, Charles Olson.

In the early 1960s, he joined poet Jonathan Williams traveling by foot throughout England. He also participated, during this period, in the concrete poetry movement, becoming a close friend with poet-artist Ian Hamilton Finaly.

In 1968 he moved to San Francisco, where he has lived for most of the years since except brief periods when he taught at the University of Kentucky in 1971 and the University of Washington in 1973.

His most important book is Ark, collected and published in 1996 by Living Batch Press. Among his other important works are The Book of the Green Man (1967), Eyes and Objects (1976), and RADI OS I–IV (1977). Sun & Moon Press will collect his complete RADI OS WORKS as The Outworks in late 1998.

Johnson died while this volume was in preparation.

Pentti Saarikoski

from *Trilogy*
Translated from the Finnish by Anselm Hollo

XIV

   the harmony of the evening
equals the balance of terror within me
but the peace of the mountains

We plant roses with wrinkly leaves
and the cat walks along the stone fence to see
if there is anything in her bowl

Facets of days
I sat in the fish harbor on the pier
looked at boats listened to water
the water's glint of silver and gold
was this arrival
was I permitted to stay here

One has to write a little about everything
or everything about a little

But the peace of the mountains is not threatened
caves and tunnels were dug into them
and they do suffer
but the peace is deeper

I sat in a café
imagined what these people will be doing
after they've eaten
what they will do tonight

they have been taught to read
to understand edicts better
they have been taught to write
so they can fill out forms
but what will they do for you, at night, tonight?

the radio reports the bowing and scraping
of Finland's communists
the bowing and scraping of Italy's
yes the communists of the west
demand the right to bow and scrape
to whatever trend they choose
can one retain one's integrity
when one is integrated?
The Vietnam war is over
after I last wrote about it
there have been changes
in the relationships between nations
or are those just seasonal

So many convictions buried in the Kremlin wall
but only propaganda
is true

Here I have watched the construction
of a supermarket
woe unto us when they truly
start serving us!
for that war, our roses are
scant armaments
the small creatures of the yard
poor soldiers

The evening's harmony
equals the balance of terror within me
but peace lies deeper, the peace of the mountains
is in no jeopardy

XV

 When raindrops are blood, heaven grieves
It
fucked my daughter
while I was out looking for mushrooms
and now Sarpedon
is dead

I got a horse
that had wings and flew

This time of year mushrooms can be found
on the hillside by bending back the grasses
In the city of Alexandria there are scholars
who trace their lineage to me
that is the custom
of the academies of logographers

But I ventured, presented
fatal signs
received a horse an airplane
wanted to meet the gods for lunch
but froze, froze
before I reached that table

My name my cradle
golden cradle
all generations
back to Mycenae!

heaven
is a swan's beak and a bull, is
fog and obfuscation. Then I entered the house
where someone had died, left his pants on a nail

XVI

Not to forget childhood, the war reparations
but they have been paid

How the trees speak to me, the wind in the grass
night warm along my cheek
Always the nights have been dear to me
intervals between days, the dermis
The waters

and trees, against leaden sky
the grey-green velvet of an excited cunt
One has to be cruel to oneself
we are in a trap, charity won't help us
criticism is impossible
cut! cut!
In the morning light
suddenly
everything may wither
and we are poor
light treacherous fires on sandbanks
dream of a golden cradle
eat the bitter root, tell lies
Who owns the land whence you came?
who the dirt you will be?

The trees betray me but not the wind
The God of Israel has led me astray

When my ship goes down
an echo rolls through the sky

One of the major Finnish poets of the Twentieth Century, Pentii Saarikoski was the spokesman through the early 1970s for what European literary historians now call the "Generation of '68." As a highly literate and iconoclastic radical in a "buffer zone" country whose political climate in the Cold War years presented great ambiguities, he was, for a time, an idol of the youth. The popular press referred to him as "The Blond Beatle of the North" — a role to which he contributed by his scandalous public behavior and pronouncements and his introduction into Finnish of major translations such as Ulysses and The Catcher in the Rye. His books from the period, Out Loud, The Red Flags, and I Look Out Over Stalin's Head reveal his public engagement. He became the editor of a literary and cultural journal sponsored by one of Finland's Marxist parties, but was relieved of that post after publishing the the first Finnish translations of Ezra Pound in the journal's inaugural issue. Throughout these years Saarikoski enjoyed his fame, spending much of his time in the Helsinki bar Kosmos where he drank heavily; he also married four times, fathering five children.

In 1962 he wrote the important essay, Mitä tapahtuu todella (What Is Really Going On), which has been described as the first "postmodern" Finnish poem, and which was a sort of "structural blueprint," as translator Anselm Hollo calls it, for his magnum opus, Trilogy. His Collected Poems was published in 1978. Saarakosi died in August 1983.

Anselm Hollo is the author of several books of poetry including Pick Up the House, Outlying Districts, and Corvus. Born in Finland, he settled in the United States in 1966. An award winning translator, Hollo lives in Boulder, Colorado, where he teaches at the Naropa Institute.

COMMENTARY

Jacques Roubaud

"About"

Translated from the French by Guy Bennett

It has long been known that poets don't know what they're saying. They say one thing then they say the opposite.

You can't count on them, a fact Socrates pointed out years ago, one that even school children know, and that I've been able to confirm by experience.

I practice a particular artistic discipline, not really plastic, not really musical, although it has its similarities with music, yet also occasionally comprises visual and graphic investigations: it is *poetry*, a modest sector and, let's be honest, somewhat neglected in the contemporary world, of the LANGUAGE ARTS. On this account I'd like to relate the personal experience of a meeting between a practitioner of poetry, myself, and a class in a Parisian elementary school.

A few years ago, I wrote a little book of poems intended for a public of all ages (but children in particular) called *Everybody's animals* (and published, with illustrations by Marie Borel and Jean-Yves Cousseau, by Seghers). Each poem was about a more or less familiar animal, one that pretty much everybody knew—the dormouse, the hedgehog, the otter, the duck, the (pink) elephant, the junebug, the giraffe, the snail…beginning with the cat (but without the dog).

A little later, once the book had made its way into bookstores and reached a few schools, I received a letter from a young man of 7 or 8 years of age, a third grade student, if my memory serves me right, which began something like this:

Hello Jacques Roubaud,
My name is Etienne and I'm learnin some of your poems in my school. The teacher has already taught us: The poem of the cat, the rhinosceros, the dinosaurs, the snaile (an *e*, crossed

out, I respect the spelling of the letter—J.R.), the marmot and that's all.

Last week my dad told me that he went somewhere wher you read some poems with your friend Pierre l'artigue (he's his friend too). I didn't believe him cause I thought you lived at the same time as Victor Hugo.

Having learned from his father that I was a living poet, an endangered species, as we know, one that he thought had disappeared from the face of the earth like dinosaurs and dodos, young Etienne had an idea. His letter went on more or less like this: If you are (really) alive (in spite of his father's affirmation to the contrary, he had a lingering doubt, which could only be dispelled, in accordance with the sound doctrine of the experimental sciences, in one way: by verification of fact), so if you are alive, Etienne L. wrote me, come to my school. my teacher, Miss S., says it's OK. I'll be waiting for you.

He added the address of his school and, as a precaution, already dubious of the practical abilities of poets, indicated that when I got to the school I was to press a button that would open the door, that I should cross the courtyard, go up two flights of stairs, take the corridor to the left (or was it to the right, I don't recall exactly), and go to the third class. That would be the one.

Having made an appointment with the teacher, I went to Etienne's school, answered questions from the little girls and boys in the class, and read the poems they wanted to hear. One of the poems was about the pigeons of Paris, an unsavoury bunch. I hesitated and asked them why they wanted me to read that particular poem; after a quick glance at Miss S., one boy said "because it has 'bad words'." The poem, which I read with the permission of Miss S. (who assured me that she was making an exception in my case) did in fact begin like this:

The pigeons that shit on Paris
Its trees, its benches, its automobiles
Can't wait till the Hôtel de Ville
is clean so they can cover it with piss.

Later in our meeting I had, on reading a poem dedicated to the cow (and that I shall reproduce here in its entirety), a very interesting lexical and zoological discussion which will serve as the moral to this little experiment in the contact of two spheres: the didactic sphere, and the far removed sphere of the irresponsible inventor of poetry.

The Cow

The
Cow
Is
An

Animal
That
Has
About

Four
Legs
That

Reach
To
The ground.

Having read the poem (it's a sonnet), I sensed that something in the portrait of this particular animal bothered some of my listeners. It turned out to be the word "about." We discussed (with the aid of Miss S.) the meaning of this word for a time, and when it was clear for every one, their disapproval was unanimous: "why do you say 'about,' Jacques?" they said to me (it didn't take long for them to call me by my first name), "a cow's got four legs!" "really," I responded, "how do you know, have you counted them?" Certain children had. I told them that since I hadn't counted the legs of each and every cow, I couldn't be sure that they all had the same number of legs. Maybe somewhere, in Savoy for example, there were some with five, or even three legs. I told them that cows were big animals and that you couldn't always see all their legs together at the same time and that, as a result, it was difficult to count them; that's why, as a precaution, not to say something wrong, I had written "about." They still didn't agree: a cow's got four legs and that's that! We discussed it further but couldn't come to a conclusion. And finally, seeing my obstination and lack of precision they turned to Miss S. and said: "How many legs does a cow have?" "Four," answered Miss S.... "Told you so!" they said.

Born in 1932, Jacques Roubaud is one of the major contemporary writers of France. Among his numerous collections of poetry are Σ (Gallimard, 1967), *Trente et un au cube* (Gallimard, 1973), *Autobiographie, chapitre 10* (Gallimard, 1977), *Les Animaux de tout le monde* (Ramsay, 1983), *La Pluralité des mondes de Lewis* (Gallimard, 1991, published in the US by Dalkey Archive Press), and *Monsieur Goodman rêve de chats* (Folio Cadet or, 1994). *The essay above is taken from* Poésie, etcetera: ménage, *published by Éditions Stock in 1995; it will appear as a Green Integer book in early 1999.*

Vicente Huidobro

Manifesto Mayhaps
Translated from the French by Gilbert Alter-Gilbert

There's no sure path and poetry is skeptical of itself.

So? the search goes on.

My nerves jangled not by a guitar or by restlessness, but by a thing which had its conception far away inside a poem, I saw snow flying about the pole, and pipesmoke swirling about a sailor.

A few days later, I perceived, the pole was a pearl for my cravat.

And the Explorers?

They became poets and stood singing above their waves of verse.

And the Poets?

They had become explorers and sought crystals in the gullets of nightingales.

This is why the Poet is equivalent to a Globe-Trotter with an active metier, and the Globe-Trotter is equivalent to a Poet without a passive metier.

Above all, he must sing or simply speak, without obligatory equivocation, but of some sort of vague discipline.

No fictive elevation, only the true, which is organic. Let's leave the sky to the astronomers, the cellules to the chemists.

The poet is not a telescope changeable into its contrary, and if the star collides against the eye in the interor of the tube, that is not a matter of magnification, but of the lens of the imagination.

Not of machine or of modernity in itself. Neither of gulf stream nor of cocktail, because the gulf stream and the cocktail have become more of a machine than a locomotive or a diving bell, and more modern than New York and its catalogs.

Milan…naive city, weary virgin of the Alps, virgin just the same.

AND THE GREATEST DANGER TO THE POEM IS THE POETIC

I tell you we must search elsewhere, far from the machine and from the dawn, as far from New York as from Bizance.

Don't add to poetry that which is already there without need of you. To pour honey over honey is nauseating.

Let the sun dry the smoke of factories and the tear-stained hankies of farewell.

Place your slippers in the moonlight, and afterwards we will speak of it and, most of all, do not forget that Vesuvius, in spite of futurism, is full to bursting with Gounod.

And as for the unforeseen?

Doubtless it would be a thing which presents itself with the impartiality of a gesture born of chance, and not really wished for, but it's uncomfortably close to instinct and more animal than human.

Chance is fine when deuces count the same as five aces or a least a royal flush. Otherwise, it must be excluded.

The poem should not be drawn from lots, nor does the poet's desktop have a cover of green felt.

And if the best poem can be made in the throat, this is because the throat is the midpoint between the heart and the brain.

Make poetry, but don't beat around the bush. Invent it.

The poet must not be an instrument of nature, but will make nature his instrument. That is the only difference from the old schools.

Here you come now bringing a new fact, all simple in its essence, independent of all external phenomena, a human creation, very pure and worked out by the brain with the patience of an oyster.

Is it a poem, or something else?

It's of little importance.

Little importance that the creature be a girl or a boy, or that he or she will be a lawyer, engineer, or biologist, so long as they be.

This endures and troubles, even while remaining at bottom very calm.

It is perhaps not the conventional poem, but it is just the same.

Thus, the first effect of the poem, the tranfiguration of our daily Christ, disarmingly naive, his big eyes open to the edges of melting words, his brain descending to his chest and heart climbing to his head, and all the rest of heart and brain, with their essential faculties, in total revolution. The earth spins backwards, and the sun rises in the west.

Where are you?

Where am I?

The cardinal points are lost in a heap, like four aces shuffled in a pack of cards.

Afterwards, one loves or one refuses, but the illusion has been couched on some commodious chairs, boredom has caught a good train, and the heart has overturned its flagon of unconscionable smells.

Love or its refusal are of no importance for the true poet, because he knows that the world marches from right to left and that men go from left to right. That is the law of equilibrium.

And so my hand guides you to the desired passages and causes a stream to be born from an almond tree without jabbing a spear in its side.

And when the dromedaries of your imagination want to disperse themselves, I stop them cold, swifter than a thief in the desert.

So that they won't wander about in directionless promenades!

The Bourse of Life.

That is clean, that is clear. No personal interpretation.

Life is Life and the Bourse is the Bourse.

Each verse is the point of an angle which closes on itself, not the disjunction of an angle which opens itself to the winds.

The poem, as it is presented here, is not realist, but human.

It isn't realist, but it becomes reality.

Cosmic reality with its own atmosphere and land and water, just as land and water own all the words on which they front.

There is no point searching these poems for the memory of things seen, nor for the possibility of seeing others.

A poem is a poem, just as an orange is an orange and not an apple.

You will not find things which exist in advance of it nor direct contact with objects outside of it.

The poet will no longer imitate nature, because he is not accorded the right to plagiarize God.

Thenceforward you will find what you have never seen elsewhere: the poem. A creation of man.

And of all human forces, that which interests us the most is the force of creation.

Born in Santiago, Chile in 1893, Vicente García Fernández (Vicente Huidobro) was educated at a Jesuit school, which later led to a profound spiritual crisis in the young man, as he revolted against his aristocratic Roman Catholic upbringing. He left for Paris in 1916, having published six books of poetry. Although the first four books had little new to offer, he had moved in the last years of his youth to develop the ideas, most clearly in Adán, *which in Paris Pierre Reverdy, Huidobro and others would describe as "creationism."*

Once in Paris, Huidobro (the pseudonym he had created for himself) began to contribute to the avant-garde literary magazines, pariculary Sic *and* Nord-Sud, *which he co-edited with Reverdy and Guillaume Apollinaire. During these early years he published six further books of poetry, including* Horizon Carré, Tour Eiffel, *and* Hallali. *Travel to Madrid in 1918 brought the attention of the Spanish avant-gardists such as Gerardo Diego, Juan Larrea, and Jore Luis Borges, who encouraged him. The result of this interchange was Ultraism, which would, in turn, influence the young Argentine poet, Oliverio Girondo.*

Huidobro returned to Chile for one year in 1925 and became the editor of a newspaper and ran as candidate for the Chilean Federation of Students in the national elections. Upon his defeat, he returned to France, where he continued his writing, publishing works in several genres, including fiction and other genres. It was in this same year that he wrote Manifestes, from which the work above was taken.

In 1936 he participated in the Spanish Civil War on the side of the Republic. As the fall of the Republic became imminent, he returned to Chile, where he wrote his important satirical novel, Sátiro; o, el ponder de las palabras (1939).

Huidobro's major poetic work was his long poem, Altazor, subtitled "Journey in a Parachute," published in Madrid in 1931. Like Joyce and other major avant-gardists, Huidobro's work is made up a of a complex layering of word-play and puns. Even the title relates to the root words: alto (high), Asor (goshawk), while at the same time, through its subtitle, suggesting the Icarus-like possibilities of the fall.

He died in Cartagena in 1948.

Gilbert Alter-Gilbert has translated many works from the Spanish and French. His translation of Huidobro's Manifest/Manifestoes will appear from Green Integer in 1998. He has also translated a collection of tales by Alberto Savinio which Sun & Moon Press will publish next year.

Takahashi Mutsuo

The Poem of 1999
Translated from the Japanese by Hiroaki Sato

When we entered the 1990s, we entered in fact, in our perception, the year 1999. We did so in the first one-tenth of what would, by the way of counting till then, last for ten years. To put it differently, there could only be the year 1999 after 1989. And what comes next is the year 2000.

*

Circumspectly speaking, the twentieth century lasts until the year 2000 and the twenty-first century begins in the year 2001. But the year 2000 is also the beginning of the 2000s. In our perception, the century, which has the figure 19 for its first two digits, ends in 1999. The year 1999 is the dead end, the edge of a cliff for this century. And its dead end began as soon as the year 1989 came to an end.

*

The dead end, the edge of a cliff for a century occurred a hundred years ago as well: 1899. Did the year 1899, as in the case of 1999, come after 1889 and last for the duration of ten years? The answer is no. Following 1889 came 1890, then 1891, which was followed consecutively by 1892…and next to 1898 came 1899. And 1900.

*

It is said that the notion of a "century" appeared first around the twelfth century in Europe and the notion of "the end of the century" was invented in the nineteenth century. Here, too, we might speculate that people were shocked by the thought that the numeral 19 topping the word "century" was to change to 20, from the teens to the twenties. This shock spawned the notion of "the end of the century," we might say, which hadn't existed before then.

*

However, the end of the previous century is essentially different from that of this century. To be sure, at the end of the previous century, too, there were a number of prophecies full of anxieties about the end of the world. But it in the end stayed within the boundaries of *atmosphere*. In contrast, the prophecy for the end of the world at the end of this century is one clearly underpinned with scientific calculations. Prophecy…perhaps I should correct it to say forecast.

*

One example of such calculations is population. The global population for some time has been doubling every thirty years. It is said that if such doubling continues, before another 2,000 years pass, the weight of mankind on earth will be equal to the weight of the earth itself. The figure 2,000 is important. It is about 2,000 years from the legendary birth of Jesus Christ, which is the starting point of the notion of a "century" and therefore of "the end of the century," until today. Even before the extension of the same length of time of 2,000 years is reached in the future, the weight of mankind reaches that of the earth… Imagine an apocalyptic image of the earth, unable to sustain that weight, falling in acceleration through the darkness of the universe along with the human beings who, piling up in tens and hundreds of layers, have rendered its surface invisible.

*

Of course, even if the population continues to double, human beings can't possibly live until that happens. Just thinking about food, which is the minimum condition for human survival, mankind will find it difficult to survive another hundred years, no, even fifty years. The end of the century we lived today may well be the last end of the century mankind experiences.

*

Despite this forecast, human beings are continuing to give birth to their own duplicates, children. In addition, they are continuing to increase the embodiments of their desires such as cars, airplanes, and computers. From another angle, this is to say they are continuing to destroy nature. That is, they are bringing the end of mankind closer. And to finish it up, there are nuclear bombs. The hypothesis that this *might* be the last end of the century is becoming infinitely close to the assertion that it *must* be.

*

There should naturally be rebuttals to the forecast so described. The most optimistic say that before the decisive crisis arrives, much of mankind will move to colonize other stars. Even the most pessimistic say that large-scale wars and slaughters will occur, killing most of mankind, allowing small portions to survive, thereby enabling the age of man to continue. Either way, it is a new theory of the Ark.

*

There is another optimsitic view. It is the theory that points to the increases in the number of both men and women who remain unmarried and do not procreate, and says that this is a natural brake on rapid population increases. There is also a different kind of report. It says that the number of spermatozoa in men's sperm in industrialized countries has decreased by half in the past fifty years. If this condition accelerates, as it is expected to, the result will be an impossibility, not far into the future, of procreation through normal intercourse between man and woman. This is precisely nature's response to rapid population increases, and this phenomenon will gradually spread, it says, from industrialized to developing countries. If this is the case, we'll have to add to this the emergence of AIDS and other viruses.

*

In any case, in the sense that the end of mankind has become a distinct possibility underpinned by scientific calculations, not as an *atmosphere*, the end of this century is essentially different from the end of the previous century. It is in this sense that I said earlier that when we entered the 1990s, we had in fact entered the year 1999. Well then, in the year which is the dead end, the edge of a cliff where we can see the end of mankind, what meaning does poetry have?

✳

Etymologically, poetry *(=poésie)* means to make *(=poiêsis poieó)*. At this edge of a cliff for mankind, what does this making mean? If to "make" in this sense is no different from to "make" cars, airplanes, and computers, not to mention nuclear bombs, doing so will contribute to the destruction of nature, bringing the end of mankind closer. Even if we are to limit ourselves to simple phenomena, to make a thousand copies of a book of poems means to destroy trees and other parts of nature that a thousand copies of a book of poems require and to deprive nature of the space to be occupied by those thousand copies.

✳

There may be an opinion that making poetry is essentially different from making cars and computers. Some will say that it is similar to growing rice and breeding cattle. But agriculture and cattle-breeding were originally *natural* and were, if anything, of a *secondary* nature; to be more exact, they were the first attempts at nature destruction. Who can say making cars and computers is not modern-day agriculture and cattle-breeding?

✳

Needless to say, there may be an opinion that making poetry is essentially different from growing rice and breeding cattle. Rice and cattle have shape and bulk just as cars and computers do; in contrast, poetry doesn't. Poetry is above all spiritual, and a book of poems is no more than a temporary material manifestation. But one can also argue that cars and computers are equally spiritual at the stage of ideas and what we see are no more than temporary material forms.

✳

It does not seem that there is a spiritual and material distinction in making. Making is originally spiritual, and the result of the spirit wanting shape and making use of material may be rice as an agricultural product, a cow as a cattle-breeding product; or else, it may be a car, a computer. The same can be said of poetry making. Making poetry is originally spiritual, and the result of that spirit wanting shape and making use of material is a poem (=poème). A poems is material even when it does not take the form of a book of poems but is simply written on a white sheet of paper because white paper and ink are material; it is material even when it is not written down but is only uttered in a voice because a voice is material; it is material even when it is simply memorized because memory is material.

*

However, what we have to be concerned about is not material so much as the spirit. For the spirit is a human invention and it is the ultimate culprit for changing nature in its natural state and destroying it. What is nature in its natural state? It is—though this, too, is according to our spirit's analysis—the universe that was born out of nothingness as a result of the Big Bang, and has, in the process of its growth, spawned the solar system, the earth, and life, separate mankind from that life, and will in due time decline either through expansion or contraction, in the end returning to nothingness. Nature, even when left to its own devices, declines and heads toward nothingness. In this process mankind or the spirit merely destroys it and hastens its own annihilation by attempting to revise in order to make its own circumstances as comfortable as possible. If the act of making is at the center of the spirit's work, a poem is no exception.

*

I have just said that the spirit is a human invention; more precisely, though, I should say that it branched out of mankind which branched out of life. Just as mankind that branched out of life sacrifices life for its own comfort, so does the spirit that branched out of mankind sacrifice mankind for its own comfort. Viewed this way, we can more easily understand the present circumstances in which we can foreseee the end of mankind. Is not the spirit trying to survive at the expense of mankind? —Even though the consequence will in fact lead to the annihilation of the spirit itself.

✳

What will directly annihilate the spirit? In logical order, it has to be poetry (=making) which branched out of the spirit. Poetry annihilates the spirit, then mankind…then life itself, or will it? Life, even left alone, will grown, then decline, and ultimately return to nothingness. As I have already pointed out, mankind will sacrifice life out of its egoism, but life's return to nothingness as a result of that sacrificing will be partial for the time being. For before then mankind will perish.

✳

If after mankind has perished, the spirit that branched out of mankind stays, and after the spirit has perished, the poetry that branched out of the spirit stays, that which will destroy poetry will have to be something that branches out of poetry. What will branch out of poetry? It will ultimately be nothingness—nothingness that will branch out of poetry before the end of life, of the earth, and probably of the universe.

✳

My thinking has come thus far, but I in fact stay put. My initial expectation was a vague one that at the present point in time where there is only despair for the future, I might still be able to find hope in poetry. As a result of deduction, however, I have reached the opposite place. So now, what can I do? Let's try to go back to the starting point.

✳

Yet, the starting point must always be nothingness. Besides, here there may be some unexpected hope. We talk of nothingness, but the fact is that we don't know nothingness. Nothingness, on the contrary, might take poetry, the spirit, mankind, life, the earth, the universe to the non-material "other shore" where multiplication does not interfere with the others. If from the edge of a cliff of the year 1999, beyond the spectacle of the end of mankind we can see the spectacle of nothingness branching out of poetry (which a brain scientist might explain from the viewpoint of material change—or, shall we say, transformation—that goes beyond the brain's imagination), we will be witnessing a picture more moving than that of the infant Jesus Christ branching out of the legendary Virgin Mary.

Born in Yahata, Kyushu in 1937, Takahashi Mutsuo spent most of his early youth with relatives and other families, his father having died soon after his birth. With the end of World War II, he began to write poetry, publishing his first book of poetry, Mino, My Bull, *in 1949. During that same period Takahashi became friends with Friar Tsuda, and became interested in Catholicism. He graduated from Fakuoka University of Education in 1962.*

From the beginning, Takahashi's poetry was overtly homosexual, and his second book, Rose Tree, Fake Lovers, *published in 1964, has been compared to the writings of Walt Whitman and Allen Ginsberg. The same year, he became acquainted with Japanese novelist Yuko Mishima, with whom he was to remain friendly until Mishima's suicide in 1970.*

Over the next several years, Takahashi published numerous books of poetry, fiction, and essays, including Dirty Ones, Do Dirtier Things; Twelves Perspective, Ode; Holy Triangle, *and* King of the Calendar. *He also traveled extensively to many countries; his work has been translated into a number of languages; five books have appeared in English, all translated by Hiroaki Sato.*

In the 1970s Takahashi worked with translations of Greek and French literature, published a magazine, Symposium, *and continued his travels, this time to San Francisco, Germany, Austria, Hong Kong, and Algeria. He recently traveled to Columbia to appear in the Mendellín International Poetry Festival. A long work he wrote about that experience will appear in the next issue of* Mr. Knife, Miss Fork.

Will Alexander
The Caribbean: Language as Translucent Imminence

Language being the primal conductor of liberty becomes the magnetic barometer of the primary link between the salubrious psyche and the world in which it exists. It carries in its wake a fervour, a confidence, a pronation, like a perpetual monsoon tree dialectically consumed and utopian, so that bondage to an inferior magnetic is broken and one is freed to explore the lingusitic realms protracted through the turbulence of one's identity. In the Caribbean identity has been none other than the suppressed African content of speech. The deprecated rotation, the subtractive kinetic, continuously devitalized by the Metropolitan psyche as it advances its tenets from London, or Amsterdam, or Paris.

In the Caribbean the slavers' most lasting form of power has been their hold over language, their mesmeric dispensation to the African diaspora concerning the latter's collective debasement, and their status at the bottom of the human order. The French, the Dutch, the English, the Spanish, from the first debacle of capture, brutally imparted a psycho-physical alienation upon the African identity, so that every person of color was haunted by a definitive self-hatred. One's identity was then contorted by values which effectively inscribed upon the mind a particular and incontrovertible image combined by failure, alienation, and barbarity. One's self assertion was thereby withdrawn, and no reason or ambition could persist. One was simply a tool to be used to the greater good of a European economy based upon one's neglect and impalement.

So when these standards were thoroughly internalized and repetitively recodified, generations emerged replete with self-imposed doubt, crippled by a punitive self-stalling negation. One then exists by means of alien definitives, by charismatic benchmarks, which label one's worth as the lesser darker property, capable of occupying nothing more than the level of a despicable, nefarious misfit. A contemptible adjective incapable of possessing a necessitious moral vigor, which would spur one's self-governing ability. In consequence, there is always instruction from the racial elite as regards how best to tailor one's day to day needs, restricted as they are to the sullen discord of the bestial. Injustice becomes one's daily metier carried out with the blessing of a hierarchy condoned by the Judeo-Christian diety.

Under such circumstance all stamina is tested in every hamlet of occupation, be it Monserrat or Barbados or Guadeloupe, all possessions of greater Europe. Therefore, what the person of color represents is what the Cuban Retamar calls "the culture of Caliban." "Caliban is thus the fear-object and savage slave of the Western psyche, the dream-evil that terrorizes the night play of timid, fair-skinned Western children." As George Lamming puts it: "Caliban is excluded, that which is eternally below possibility and always beyond reach. He is seen as an occasion, a state of existence which can be appropriated and exploited for the purposes of another's own development. Caliban is a reminder of lost virtue or the evil vigor of the Beast that is always there: a magnetic temptation, an eternal warning against the contagion of his daemon ancestry." Lamming continues, profoundly understanding that "Caliban should be embraced as the continuing possibility of a profound revolutionary change initiated by Toussaint L'Ouverture in the Haitian war of independence."

So by making a leap, by embracing one's African eclipse sun, one casts out the ideal of Metropolitan acculturation, moving in harmony with an African inner rhythm, no longer naively ingesting facts which Aimé Cesaire mocks, such as the reign of "Queen Blance of Castile," or, say, in an English-speaking confine being subject to such niggling datum as the death of Queen Victoria and the accession of Edward the VII to the throne. Such details become neglibible, obsolescent, to be kicked about like a dishonored corpse over stones.

Of course, such previous assertion has not always been the case. If I were a British subject in Barbados at the beginnng of the 1930s, for example, I would perhaps be incapable of understanding the seminal undermining of Toussaint's Haiti by Western trade block-ade. I would subconsciously attribute Toussaint's failure to the darkness of his integument, which would equate in my mind with an inherent lack of stewardship. I would then look into the mirror and confirm my thesis by the impoverished state of my own esteem. Self-defeat would allow me to understand only within the context of the region's superficial historicity. I could account for the settlement of Barbados by the English in 1627; I could mention in passing that Monserrat was christened by Columbus and colonized by Irish settlers in 1632; or inadvertant lucidity would bring forth the fact that in 1648 Saint Martin was partitioned by the French and the Dutch. As to any intrinsic speculation concerning revolt or defiance, none would occur. Nothing in the neural field would vibrate, my electric nest of spiders would condense in self-imposed blankness. No psychic concurrence with the blood of Dahomey, with the mirculous powers of Timbuktu.

So, when Césaire breaks away from mulatoo salons in Paris, and concentrates on linguistic return to high Africa, the scenario I just described is irreparably rent by means of a ferocious seditionary language, by means of intense verbal scaupers, tearing down the veneer of the complexity of self-hatred; and what emerges from his Antillean powers is the "turbulent poetry" of magnetic cyclone trees. He then rings by means of language the bell of self-contact, thereby connecting the visible with the invisible, conspicuity with concealment. By means of the dialectic he becomes capable of mining an African neural Eden where purpose and meaning are electrically revealed, impowered by the flames of vertiginous fecundity. Melanin then becomes psycho-physical empowerment no longer squared by Euro-centric distortion. When, like Césaire, one comes to such interior fruition, one no longer fields dictates from the British or the French concerning the depth of one's telluric designation.

Yet the point is well taken when Siméa, the mother of principal narrator Marie-Gabriel, "remonstrates with Suzanne Cesaire" in Daniel Maximin's novel *Lone Sun*. Seeing her native Gaudeloupe in the same degree as she does her neighbor Martinique, she finds fault with Madame Césaire for so heavily consulting Frobénius, a "white ethnologist" on things African. But what Siméa or other critics must understand is that a start was made in the Tropiques, an African motor principle was acknowledged. Yes, a certain threshold was crossed, a certain amplitude was heightened as regards the African diaspora and the nobility of its origin.

From the genesis of this fortuitous spark, it became possible to open to the homocentric context of ancient Ghana, of Songhai, of Mali. By such opening as Négritude provided there was organic access to, say, the mathematical and astronomical genius of the Dogon people. Black people who "knew the rings of Saturn," of "the four principle moons of Jupiter," and "the rotundity of the earth and its turning on its axis." Even more astoundingly, they knew of the intricate details of the Sirius star system, of Sirius's "approximate mass," of its axial rotation, of its orbital period. All of this known for at least five hundred years, five hundred years throughout which the European propagandists berated the African mind as having procured no intrinsic achievment. We are told by this spurious assumption that peoples such as the pygmies of the Ituri Forest were at the opposite pole of human sensibility. Yet it has been revealed that, without any recourse to modern instrumentation, they knew of the nine moons of Saturn. With the rise of Négritude movement, it became understood that the use of one's own language provided an illuminant umbilical connecting the past to the crucial complexities of the future.

What the future represents are the voices, like Daniel Maximin or Edouard Glissant, or Franz Fanon. They create a tenor for the person of color to make an orphic descent into and out of the "pit of interiority" so as to recover and facilitate a Black psychic force, thereby dissolving by this movement alienation as a given. From this orphic act, a surge transpires in which European classification takes on the character of a disrupting anomaly. For this reason there is now the uncontested ability of the Caribbean writer to take liberty as a given, where one is no longer "thought by others." Language becomes a heritage of complexity, not a mechanical placement of steps, but a thing infused by a perplexity of plentitude, in which to be "part European does not necessarily mean to be assimilated, to lose one's racial and cultural identity." Thus the Antillean personality ceases to reel within the throes of a peripheral cul de sac, with suppositious values drawn from pernicious incitement by European inhibition, which sees the mind as the last battlefield of suggestion. In this too the former colonizers have in the long term failed. Take for example the collective quote from the Antillean writers Jean Bernabé, Patrick Chamoiseau, and Raphaël Confiant:

> It was Césaire's Négritude that opened to us the path
> or the actuality of a Caribbeanness which from then on
> could be postulated, and which itself is leading to
> another yet unlabelled degree of authenticity. Césairian
> Négritude is a baptism, the primal act of our restored
> dignity. We are forever Cesaire's sons.

Even if the critic Bernadette Cailler criticizes Daniel Maximin's *Lone Sun* for failing to achieve the combination "between poetry and history," I think one can safely say that the book would not carry its present predilection were it not for the pioneering bravery of the poets Damas and Césiare. By their acts, the Rubicon of "intellectual poverty" was crossed, putting language in contact with the "primordial," and the "multivalent."

By plunging into orphic turblence Césaire withdrew his words from "utilitarian usage," thereby "disalienating them and restoring…to his Black people, their original state of possibilities, their state of 'virtualite.'" Because of this all things persist in the connivance of liberty. The flora, the fauna, the lyrical botany of the atmosphere can be described as a "perfectly green sea" under "a prodigious orange light." The tellurian powers taken on an enthralling force of grammar, where tornadoes cast spells, where the native gecko takes on the power of a noctambulent radiance.

The Antilles—truly south of the American South—where unlike the diaspora to the north, its inhabitants at present both enjoy a psychic as well as numerical advantage, and exists for me as a hidden ark for both present and future African concatenation from which a beacon mesmerically burns with the stars of a translucent imminence.

American poet Will Alexander is the author of Asia and Haiti *(Sun & Moon Press, 1995) and* The Stratospheric Canticles *(Pantograph Press, 1995) as well as other books. He lives in Los Angeles.*

REVIEWS

[*Mr. Knife, Miss Fork* regularly reviews new titles in English and English translation, but also invites short reviews of books of poetry when they first appear in their original language. Sun & Moon books are mentioned with short quotations from backcover copy or poems.]

American Poetry

Jeff Clark. *The Little Door Slides Back.* Los Angeles: Sun & Moon Press, 1998. 112 pages. $10.95

One of the five books selected for the 1996 National Poetry Awards, this is San Francisco poet Jeff Clark's first book publication. Selector Ray DiPalma wrote of the book: "In characterizing the poems in *The Little Door Slides Back*, a predictable compliment of adjectives might enthusiastically embrace the dark music of this fine book: well-crafted, resonant, intelligent, and highly readable, for starters. However, the ironic threnodies, 'demonologues,' and antiphonal writing collected here afford the reader far more than a finely articulated gathering of poems. The wide-ranging and imaginatively animated expressions of self-revelation at work in these texts establish an original and confident presence, that takes its step, in part, from the visionary writings of such poets as Trakl, Desnos, and Michaux...."

*

Fanny Howe. *One Crossed Out.* St. Paul: Graywolf Press, 1997.

The blurb on the back cover of *One Crossed Out* states that the book "presents a portrait painted from the inside of the life of a homeless woman"; I was immediately and continually struck by the book's generous and forceful inclusion: the fictional woman and her acquaintances, the author, we (the reader), all together in a dialogue of meditative analysis of the common situation. No more confusing ourselves with another, we are all an other together. The duality is blown apart so that power, politics, sexuality, language, reading and writing, the exchange of ourselves through all of these include their negation equally within themselves, include all the points in between.

The question of identity and its many clues and manifestations is continually pursued in this book. Alienation and longing for a "self" outside of society's narrow interpretation and classification are beautifully portrayed during the intense experience of writing one's name: "The dot over the letter that pertains to the first person / singular is a symbol for me of my head. / I always put on my dot when I'm already out of the word." And who cannot empathize with the "storm" (internal and external) that results in "a powerless period when the word / POWER keeps repeating…." What are we, our lives and worth, in relation of our "things," in command of them or defined by them: "Apparatus, don't be embarrassed by my life / as a dishwasher…."

These poems are a cry and a relief, a description and a transcendence. "It's like she doesn't look out the window. / She looks at what's on the window." Fanny Howe doesn't go looking there but sees it HERE, vertical, aspects of consciousness all stacked up.   —*Diane Ward*

*

Ann Lauterbach. *On a Stair*. New York: Penguin (Penguin Poets), 1997.
94 pages.

No matter how ringed round with loss, the wearing effects of history, unrelenting metaphysical questions, Ann Lauterbach's poems always attend to moments of sheer radiance. They seem to swim in the vastness of time: "What is this meantime." Her most recent book, *On a Stair*, also highlights such moments, juxtaposing specific glimpses with wide-ranging abstractions:

> Something waits in the normal blue,
> a Saturday, or love, or a city besieged.
> The effects were known; they were the lived thing
> ardently collapsing into a distant litter:
> remote pages to be burned,
> the wake of a small green boat
> allotted to a scrim, or Paris,
> or Celan. How beautiful, how untrue! (from "Staircase")

The world in these poems is put into abeyance and then given back in full force, in particulars, so that the tentative and relative alternate with visual images of impressed clarity ("the bright today"). Although in "Night Barrier" she says "Father, I am deliberately/ missing the events/ by which time is told," she does not miss, but rather isolates and frames such events: "the kingfisher's plunge," "cold perfume," "crumpled/chew of a step onto snow" —all the "friction of the Given." The meaning of things, as in Derrida from whom she quotes in translation, is relative, each dependent on the context in which it is imbedded.

The title of the collection is from Emerson's essay "Experience" and thus Lauterbach's questions are also spiritual, insistent, and in this collection, somewhat more vast and rangy. In "N/est," she says: "Emerson writes, 'Where do we find ourselves. In a series of which we do not know the extremes, and believe that it has none. We wake and find ourselves on a stair; there are stairs below us, which we seem to have ascended; there are stairs above us, many a one, which go upward and out of sight.'" Immediately she refers to a poet's having to choose one word instead of another. Ann Lauterbach confronts metaphysical questions; she chooses her words with elegant precision, reaching for the confusion and awe of each separate day. — *Martha Ronk*

*

Tom Mandel. *Ancestral Cave*. Gran Canaria: Zasterle Press, 1997. 48 pages.

This charming short book by Mandel is really two longer poems, *Ancestral* and *Cave*. The first, as its title suggests, seeks out ancestral roots in the Moscow metro stations. Mandel's meditations on Russian culture, grounded in simple observation of its people in the metro, reminds one, at times, of Pound's attempt to grasp people and things in an image — albeit in another metro. But Mandel is just as interested in extrapolating ideas from his images. A woman in a living room becomes "Time in *alpha state*." Soldiers with guns, "bayonet the city." Through Mandel's transformative language, the image quickly becomes a concept, which leads to the recognition that "no person incarnates culture." It is an attempt to comprehend, to make meaning that determines what is witnessed.

The cave of the second poem is the poet's own life, begun, apparently, in his living room, and opening out, through memory and association, to his entire life. Once again, the poet explores how what is strange and disorienting (even the other of a relationship), is through language (Mandel centers this on writing) made into something that once spoken turns back to reflect upon the speaker himself. And in that sense, difference becomes, in part, self-revelation; the other is how we recognize the self. — *DM*

Fiona Templeton. *Cells of Release*. New York: Roof Books, 1997. unpaginated. $13.95

Fiona Templeton's *Cells of Release*—a book-length poem documenting a singular performance—is an absolutely unusual work of art that tries the limits of art, improvisation, performance and the political and, as with the greatest works of theater, situates the human body and voice in circumstances where its audience's presumptions are wiped away in the stream of the event.

For six weeks in the Spring of 1995, the Scottish-born, New York-based writer and performer stayed and worked on-site at Philadelphia's abandoned panopticon Eastern State Penitentiary, writing in a continuous line on a long white strip of paper—"a single prison sentence"—she wove between the cells of one block of the prison, one cell per day. Working in collaboration with Amnesty International, Templeton, in her words "dedicated each cell to a different prisoner of conscience somewhere in the world, and with the old prison furniture made the cell into a place where the visitor finds a text and photograph on each "case," and the facilities to write in petition on each prisoner's behalf.

Cells of Release, the book, is a successful translation of that performance into the space of a poem, set beside photos (by Bill Jacobson) from the prison's interior, diagrams of its chematic lay-out according to the panopticon (or "all seeing") vision of the nineteenth century British utilitarian Jeremy Bentham as suited to the American scene, and other graphics. Templeton's words, originally handwritten in one line down the center of the "endless" sheet stretched across the walls of room and corridors, are arrayed in a variously broken column down page center.

> …I can not mean by myself
> they know this
> it is their greatest weapon….

As if we could legislate our discomfort out of existence, in America it seems we're intent on criminalizing whatever behaviors frustrate what is truly an amorphous, constantly shifting picture of justice. What makes this poem an extraordinary political performance—one factor among others—is the absence of any pious regard directed at its audience. "Limits are whatever you're inside of," Charles Olson's apt phrase, finds its straightforward definition in Templeton's encounter as a writer—an encounter that is physical, psychic, intellectual—with the layers of limits anyone confronts before even the abstractions of such a thing as the "criminal justice system."

The performance Fiona Templeton undertakes is one that pierces through the abstract, peeling away the so-called insularity of the writer to find a subject and circumstance for poetry —artificial, for sure (as she knows very well, she doesn't pretend that she lives there)—but which reports to us—with the privilege of one who can write and address, at least, the outer shell —of an invisible world encased within the other world we inhabit by preference, luck, or fortune.   —Steve Dickison

*

Keith Waldrop. *The Silhouette of the Bridge (Memory Stand-Ins)*. Penngrove, California: Avec Books, 1997. 80 pages.

Keith Waldrop's *The Silhouette of the Bridge* is a fascinating mix of genres; autobiography, aphoristic journal, dream book, philosophical musings, narrative and poetry are woven together in this short text to create a strange sense of being. Waldrop's work, like the vignette with which he ends the book, is almost an apparition of a life, somehow *there*, sensed at least, almost real, but suddenly not visible. As he puts it, "I wake, unsure where I am, I and my surroundings vague, the fierce sense of reality having disappeared with the dream."

Within this almost metaphysical cunundrum, Waldrop explores memory and experience, focusing on language so attentively that "the world turns clean around between sentences or before I can decide between terms." There is, accordingly, not only a great deal of wonderment, of bemused *déjà vu* throughout the work, but the experience of a very slow building of meaning—despite the brevity of the book. Hours pass but on the clock the hands keep returning to the same number; a door is latched, but the fact is immediately forgotten, and the narrator must return to check if he has indeed locked the door. The voice of the poet despairs that time "does little but waste." The result of this slowing down of the writing process, however, is that each sentence is so carefully considered, its meaning so thoroughly explored, that what might have been mysterious and blurred in its dream-like condition, is, in fact, clearly silhouetted, outlined with an absolute vision that be it dream or not, *becomes* in the process a reality for which the poet-reader is seeking.

The poet, accordingly, may experience the world as vague, as a world in which reality has escaped into the dream, but through his incredible attention to language, we wake to find ourselves again in the concrete. The book was recently awarded the America Award for the best book of poetry in 1997.   —DM

✻

Barrett Watten. *Frame (1971-1990)*. Los Angeles: Sun & Moon Press, 1997. 336 pages. $13.95.

Frame brings together six previously published works from two decades of Watten's poetic writing: *Opera—Works, Decay, 1-10, Plasma/Parallels/"X," Complete Thought* and *Conduit*. To the older books Watten has added two previously unpublished works, *City Fields* and *Frame*.

✻ ✻ ✻

British Poetry

David Miller. *Collected Poems.* Salzburg: University of Salzburg, 1997. 110 pages.

David Miller's poems are clean, competent, and slightly unhappy with the narrative or reportorial impulse that seems to drive them; or they are cautiously "experimental" pieces that nonetheless give way to that impulse.

Both types of poems tend to present problems because they are always searching for a way back to a personal, narrative, possibly autobiographical mainstream.

> a grove of orange trees
> a silence in the midst
> of music
> shy and gentle one

Narrative carries with it its own weight of histories and conventions. These qualities are difficult to dispense with simply by using repetitions, disjunctions or interpositions of prose within a verse setting. Conversely, poems which are concerned with repetition, disjunction, and/or collaging of forms, also have specific demands. Those poetries that use both modes are successful when they deal with the contingencies that make each mode complex. This is more crucial when the overriding objective is to break away from the expectations of the more commonly received forms. There the territory is less certain, the risks greater, the prospect of recognition more dubious.

Miller does not seem to have worked this problem out. The result is poems which seem conflicted in their purpose, and which seem to return to conventionality as an automatic response to the uncertainties of the problems that he himself has laid out.

> that I loved them, & that meant
> loving them forever a small window
> that for me would be an *eternal*
> memory
> lost a darkness utterly black
> travel no visible record

This is not to say that there are not moments of acute social commentary or pleasing lyric.

> blood in the throat
> a buzzing at the lips
> eyes closed, *lids*
> of the camel's eyes
> "the flame in the
> mouth"
> eyes wide open in
> the lids
> the flame the
>
> form which cannot be spoken of
> verging on the ridiculous
> entering a room with that walk
>
> the splendour
>
> or: they wish to mutilate us
> Perched on the tree of possession.

But this work distrusts itself and engenders the same lack of trust in, at least, this reader.   — *Dennis Phillips*

Poetry in French

Oscarine Bosquet. *Chromo* (Paris: Fourbis, 1996). 56 pages.

A bright yellow cover—yellow poems—a yellow book. As Oscarine Bosquet writes in the first stanza, *Chromo* is a meditation on yellow: "je prends toutes les choses jaunes / ou pas j'emploie le mot" ["I take on all things yellow / or not I use the word."].

The work that follows is streaked with that color; it is found in every title ("Jaune observation," "Jaune dépression," "Jaune maniaque," "Jaune fiction," "Jaune almanach," etc.), and appears at least once on almost every page, presented in a variety of guises: as the yellow of certain flowers, as Pantone yellow #253, as the name of the heroine in a discontinuous, elliptical love story that runs throughout the work, or simply, as the word "yellow."

The resolutely monochrome thematicism of this book contrasts sharply with the polyform nature of the poems themselves. Written principally in verse, they are organized in stanzas of varying shapes and lengths, and are characterized by an equally diverse range of styles and techniques.

In one poem ("Jaune clinique"), passages of lyric verse alternate with minimal stanzas of anagram-like lines. These are crossed by stretches of prose filtered through subtle phonetic permutations that, like the shifting hues in a color wheel, fade from one phoeme to the next, combining and recombining into words evoking themes and images from elsewhere in the work:

> dire désir dispose do disperse dresse dépression dose dessine dense
> dos drisse dors dîne endors épode éprise en épines espion prose prédis
> pénis prends poids poésie poindre pensées pire peine près presse
> poisse pisse proie répond rose résine rein rions rosée roide répons
> repos rosse e ers eon ensis esse soir soie sinope sosie sirène soi sien
> son sein soin sine die sonde idoine irone Irène iris inde ire on orion
> onde oie ode oindre ondée ose ni noir nos

This process of phonetic reduction colors what follows, as the remaining verses of the poem collapse into themselves; lines shorten to words, words to syllables and syllables to letters, grounding the poem in language.

Chromo, the first book by Bosquet, demonstrates a penchant for formally innovative writing that explores and experiments without breaking entirely with traditional verse form. It is an imaginative, satisfying work.

—*Guy Bennett*

Alain Veinstein. *Even a Child*, translated from the French by Robert Kocik and Rosmarie Waldrop (Providence: Burning Deck, 1997). 64 pages.

Veinstein's most recent work in translation is a short trilogy about death, childhood, and love. In the first, "Introducing the Spade," the poet unsuccessfully struggles to fill space (and the hole/whole of death) with words, which, in turn, he would undo if he could as he thinks of their effect over his childhood in "Even a Child"; the third section, "An Excess Taken Back," is the strongest of the three, and in this it is almost as if he were trying to "take back" or "dig up" the grave of language which has defined and proscribed his own life (or perhaps lack of living). In this final section language becomes yet more minimal, as space, whiteness, and emptiness come to dominate. But, of course, in that white "powdery" space where there is not even a place to put his hand, he discovers himself yet closer to the "hole" of the grave with which he began.

The work as a whole, accordingly, takes on almost the quality of an elegy to a failed life, a life that cannot be relived or remade with or without language. But, obviously, is that the condition of not only the poet, but of each of our stories, stories that we live but can never understand.

—*DM*

* * *

Poetry in Italian

Luigi Ballerini. *The Cadence of the Neighboring Tribe*, translated from the Italian by Jeremy Parzen. Los Angeles: Sun & Moon Press, 1997. $10.95

A very loose translation into English of Italian poet Luigi Ballerini's *Il terzo gode* (Venice: Marsilio Editori, 1994).

> from "imitation of the dream"
>
> a poison will occur, an indulgence devoid
> of symmetry and cunning, a language will
> occur, camouflaged or slightly sculpted,
> a hypothesis of hustle and bustle, a spite
> will occur, an uphill descent (running

the risk of ruin), a sideways sing-song
will occur, a glance, an eminent vocative,
a shock of unsold recognition. Frowning
upon bequests and losing thought, a victim
of habit and mirrors, of euphoric increase

*

Elio Pagliarini. *La pietà oggetiva (Poesie 1947-1997)*, Rome: Fondazione
Piazzolla, 1997.

One of the exemplary conditions of being a modern poet is the utopia of
languages once denied many of us because of various forms of historical
privilege. In this respect, "Romanza sotto la pioggia" ("Ballad in the Rain"),
dated 1948, the second poem in the collection, brings to mind Wallace
Steven's meditation on war-ravaged Naples, "Esthétique du Mal," from
the 1947 book *Transport to Summer*. Compare one of the poem's defining
couplets, "Natives of poverty, children of malheur/ The gaiety of language
is our seigneur" (and Stevens' almost embarrassed reflections on politics
as a response to the physical world of pain and evil) to the flamboyant
opening of the young Pagliarani's postwar ballad:

> Supponiamo che io fossi nato oggi
> Con questa pioggia che mi fa cantare
> — lavorano i taxi lavorano le carrozze
> e cresce l'artrite a mio padre
>
> [Suppose I were born today
> with this rain that makes me sing
> —the taxis running the railcars running
> And my father's arthritis gaining…]

There is a certain pleasure in the fact that the 21-year-old poet's abundant,
if cranky lyricism is already an alternative to such a thoroughly skillful and
thoroughly bourgeois a writer as Stevens.

In the fifty years represented in *La pietà oggetiva*, Pagliarani's work has
remained relentless in its desire to be both clearly dependent upon and in
defiance of history. A source of his experimental exuberance (an "uninter-
rupted avant-garde," as the volume's editor Plinio Perilli calls it), the poet's
concern for lyric narration coupled with a scrupulous sense of event and

epic humor has contributed to two masterpieces of verse fiction, *La ragazza Carla* ("The Girl Carla," 1960) and *La ballata di Rudi* ("Rudy's Ballad," 1995), as well as the stunning, recitative-like collages of the 60's *Lesione di fisica e fecaloro* ("Physics Lessons and Chrysofeces," 1968), and the citation-theoretical works, *Esercizi platonici* ("Platonic Exercises, 1985) and *Epigrammi ferraresi* ("Ferrara Epigrams," 1987; readings extracted and versified from texts of Plato's dialogues and Savanarola's sermons).The verve and sweep and insistence of Pagliarani's early work with narrative culminates in *Carla:*

> allora la burasca
>> periferica, di terra,
> il ponte se lo copre e spazza e qualcheduno
> può cascar sotto
> e i film che carla non li può soffrire
> un film di Jean Gabin può dire il vero
> è forse il fischio e nebbia o il disperato
> stridere di ferrame o il tuo cuore sorpreso, spaventato
> il cuore impreparato, per esempio, a due mani
> che piombano sul petto

> [then a ground squall
>> on the outskirts,
> covers the bridge and sweeps across it and someone
> might fall below
> and the movies that Carla cannot stand them
> a Jean Gabin movie can speak the truth
> it's the whistle maybe and the fog or the desperate
> screech of iron or startled heart, a heart
> frightened and unprepared, for instance, for two hands
> that swoop on your breasts]

The "openness" of Pagliarani's work, using advisedly this precariously a-historical and mythophrenic term, is the ability of his language play to increase the scope of his vision, to better suit the subject he is trying to engage. However neo-romantic and perhaps eternally sentimental the project may seem, Pagliarani's writing learns from the things it is talking about, often contradicting itself and its lyrical passion, forcing us beyond its own inevitable limits into the experience of a world both avant-garde and ethical.

The last section of volume is dedicated to *La ballata di Rudi*, a work started more than 30 years ago, though only recently completed and published. Rich and broad in its language variations, Pagliarani's music, always corporeal, always personal and public in its attitude, may be sampled in this itinerary for those new to his long and complex career:

I problemi sociali certamente anch'io li sento forte forse voi
o credete di averli solo voi? Io do ragione a Stalin dirò di più io faccio
come lui, è da dentro che combatto, e mi funziona il mio mestire, aggancio
la gente al collo con la gioia...

> Posso spendermi solo
> per le cose che passano
> quelle che restano
> ci penserrano loro.

[Certainly I too feel the force of social problems   perhaps you
or do you think you alone have them? I think Stalin was right or better yet I'll do
like him, it's from within that I fight and what I do works for me, I catch
people by the throat with my joy...

> I can only spend myself
> on things that pass
> they can take care of
> those that last.]

—*Paul Vangelisti*

❋

Andrea Zanzotto, *Peasants Wake for Fellini's Casanova*, translated from the Italian and dialects by John P. Welle & Ruth Feldman. Champaign: University of Illinois Press, 1997

With a poet as good as Andrea Zanzotto, it is always eventful to have a new bilingual edition available. What is perplexing, however, about this new collection is that most of the volume is occupied with Zanzotto's dialect poetry. Though a fascinating and in many ways provocative part of the poet's body of work, the choice of editors and translators Ruth Feldman and John Welle to construct a book primarily composed of non-Italian writing of a major Italian poet deprives this American reader, let alone someone less familiar with contemporary Italian poetry, of the overall, innovative dimensions of Zanzotto's career.

As Feldman and Welle state in the translator's note following Welle's introduction, Zanzotto himself expressed like reservations in a 1987 letter: "presenting *only* [Zanzotto's italics] a selection of my dialect poems, without a sufficient knowledge of my other poetry, could give an imprecise idea of my work, within which the dialect is very important, but it constitutes one moment of experimentation among many others." Feldman and Welle dismiss this first objection by citing Feldman's & Brian Swann's 1975 *Selected Poetry of Andrea Zanzotto*, drawing from books published between 1951 and 1973. Beyond the fact that we are discussing editing choices and translations now at least 25 years old, these choices represented only the first half of the poet's productive life.

Also, and perhaps even more problematic, is Feldman's and Welle's choice of translating the dialect into standard English. Again they did not heed the poet's own advice: "In the translations, therefore, if the passage from Italian to English (or into another language) is already uncertain, the passage from dialect into a foreign language becomes almost impossible. The dialect *cannot* [Z.'s italics again] be rendered with Standard English. It would be necessary to find some *patois* or slang that nevertheless was rather widely known in the Anglophone area." Publishing a text that passes from neo-dialect constructions to Italian (these poems are printed *bilingually* in the Italian editions), to culminate in a rendering into standard American English of what Zanzotto's has called an "almost impossible" passage seems a truly academic exercise. Granted there is probably no American English dialect or patois with similar values to Zanzotto's use of Venetian and Solighese dialects, the translators might have tried other, more adventuresome solutions or perhaps given more serious consideration to the feasibility of this book as conceived.

Taking two opening lines almost at random, one can readily spot difficulties with *Peasant's Wake* as translation: "Toco de banda, toco de gnòca/ squínsia e barona che a nu ne tóca" (Zanzotto's dialect original)—"Pezzo di banda, pezzo di gnocca,/ civetta e traditrice che a noi càpita" (Z's Italian)—"What a dame, what a gal/ flirt and betrayer who's wished on us all." Besides the substitution of "wished on us" for the forceful sense of happenstance in the second line of both the dialect and Italian, Feldman's and Welle's grotesque, musical comedy-like euphemism of "dame" and "gal" for the explicit *banda* and *gnoca* is certainly disturbing. It points again to the problem with the entire undertaking, potentially misrepresenting, to repeat Zanzotto's warning, "one moment of experimentation among many others": some fifty years of, above all, linguistic innovation represented in a somewhat more provincial, if colorful dress.

—*Paul Vangelisti*

* * *

Poetry in Japanese

Violet Kazue de Cristoforo, Editor, Translator and Compiler. *May Sky: There Is Always Tomorrow / An Anthology of Japanese American Concentration Camp Kaiko Haiku.* Los Angeles: Sun & Moon Press, 1997. 288 pages (cloth). $29.95

This book consists of poetry written by Americans—Americans whose civil liberties were stripped in the name of defense during World War II. Violet Kazue de Cristoforo, herself a victim of the American concentration camps (as she prefers to call them) for Japanese Americans, has spent her lifetime tracking down the names and histories of the members of the original haiku clubs of Northern California, writers who continued to write haiku throughout their incarceration. This book is both a document of that experience, a testament to the spirit of the prisoners who continued artistic enterprises in the camps, and a masterful collection of amateur haiku written within the camps. The haiku are presented in their original *nihongo* (Japanese), in *romaji* (Japanese written in the Latin alphabet), and in English. Even as its publishers, we unblushingly recommend this book as one of the most interesting documents of 20th century American poetry.

*

Hayashi Fumiko. *I Saw a Pale Horse* and *Selected Poems from Diary of a Vagabond,* translated by Janice Brown (Ithaca, New York: East Asia Program, Cornell University, 1997).

This book introduces Western readers to one of Japan's most interesting poets of the 20th century. Unacknowledged by her father—which in Japan means almost complete ostracization from respectable institutions and society—Hayashi Fumiko spent most of her early life as an itinerant peddler, and upon moving to Tokyo as a young girl of nineteen, met with and participated in the circles of contemporary Japanese poetry of the

1920s. Working as a waitress and in other odd jobs, she supported herself, and forged a poetry nearly unthinkable in the Japan of her day: a partly-autobiographical oeuvre in which she dared challenge the patriarchal systems of her homeland. Her presentment of herself as an outsider, her alignment with workers and the downtrodden, fascinated the reading public and helped her to sell more than 600,000 copies of her *Diary of a Vagabond* upon its publication in the early 1930s.

Despite some dryness in a translation that focuses a bit too much on thematics as opposed to style, the marvelous originality and beauty of her poems come through in this book. Among my favorite poems are "Under the Lantern," "Taking Out the Liver," "Red Snails Gone to Sea," "Spread Out in the Sky the Cherry Tree Branches," "Stubborn, Strong," "I've Seen Fuji," "Bone of Fishbone," "Early Evening Light," and "The Fat Moon Has Vanished." But others are equally powerful. Despite her circumstances, at times desperate, there is a wry sense of humor and self-mockery in Fumiko's work. Even starvation is evoked by the images of food flying toward her:

Fly to Me, Boiled Egg

Fly to me, boiled egg
Fly to me, bean jam bun.
Fly to me, strawberry jam bread.
Fly to me, Chinese noodle soup.

At its strongest, Fumiko's poetry takes on the stock patterns of female deferment in Japanese culture, and mocks its strongest symbols, as in "I've seen Fuji," where she dismisses the symbology of the great mountain: "Mount Fuji! / Here stands a lone woman who does not lower her head to you / here is a woman laughing scornfully at you."

Brown's introduction is informative and revealing, although at times it displays the penchant of some academicians to bolster simple observations with quotations from mediocre figures. For example, Brown quotes Audre Lorde and others to explain that Fumiko took to writing poetry because of her economic condition and the little time work left her to write. But, of course, one cannot simply choose poetry as a genre like a coat; one must have the ability, the desire and the talent. And we know good poetry, particularly in the hands of a significant writer such as Fumiko is not primarily a means of quick "self-expression." Fumiko's work is important not just because it expresses a strong woman's voice speaking out in a society in which women's voices were seldom heard, but because of her ability to explore language as a tool of experience and definition, an art that takes one's whole lifetime to accomplish. —DM

*

Takahashi Mutsuo. *Selected Poems* (with a CD of his reading), translated from the Japanese by Hiroaki Sato. Tokyo: Star Valley Library, 1996.

This is the fourth book of poetry by Takahashi translated into English, and consequently, this bi-lingual edition—beautifully produced as it is—was not as exciting or satisfying for me as the 1992 publication *Sleeping, Sinning, Falling*, for example, also translated by Hiroaki Sato. *Selected Poems* contains only ten poems, several of which previously appeared in the City Lights volume. But it always a joy to read work by this wonderful writer. "Pythagoras Beans" is a very funny representation of meaningless logic:

> "Don't eat the beans,"
> our teacher said,
> "because the beans belong to the dead."
>
> "Don't eat the dead,"
> our teacher did not say,
> "because the dead belong to the beans."
>
> "Eat the dead,"
> our teacher did not say, either,
> "because the dead do not belong to the beans."
>
> "Eat beans,"
> our teacher of course did not say,
> "because the beans do not belong to the dead."
>
> "Eat your teacher,"
> the dead did not say,
> "because your teacher does not belong to the beans."
>
> ....etc.

And "Ah, Oh" and "The Monkey-Eaters" are among some of his very best of poems. Also of great interest is Takahashi's commentary about these works.   —DM

* * *

Poetry in Norwegian

Paal-Helge Haugen. *Wintering with the Light*, translated from the Norwegian by Roger Greenwald. Los Angeles: Sun & Moon Press, 1997. 96 pages. $10.95

A translation of *Det overvintra lyset* from the Norwegian, this book received the Glydendal Prize and the Nynorsk Literature Prize for the year's best book written in New Norwegian upon its original 1985 publication. Translator Greenwald has won several awards for his literary translations from the Norwegian and Swedish.

Poetry in Portuguese

Eugénio de Andrade. *Another Name for Earth / O outro Nome da Terra*, translated from the Portuguese by Alexis Levitin. Fort Bragg, California: QED Press, 1997. 110 pages. $12.95

This is the sixth book by Eugénio de Andrade that Alexis Levitin has translated into English.

The collection, divided into three parts, is driven primarily by three males, a new photographer friend of de Andrade's, Dario, a childhood friend, Gil, and Miguel, Gil's child and de Andrade's god-child. The first section, "Another Name for Earth," is accordingly addressed to childhood, to the potentiality of the future, and the fecundity associated with it. The seven poems in this section are among the book's strongest, particularly the short poem "With Apples."

> Children arrive with apples.
> They come from the south,
> the white poplars know their names.
> The sea gulls also know:
> I'll bet that's who it was,
> those gypsies of the sand,

who showed them the way.
They arrive with apples:
the children, the bees.

The second section of the book, "Complicities of Summer," is, in part, a longing for the past, for the sexual energy of de Andrade's own childhood and the loves he enjoyed. In the simple language typical of de Andrade's oeurve, the poet centers his experiences in nature, in light and sea, and the natural world in which he grew up.

The final section of the book, "Rose of the World," explores the poet's fear of and acceptance of death, ending in the angry explosion of lost beauty and hope:

Rose. Rose of the world.
Burnt.
Filthy from so many words.

First dew upon my face.
Petal by petal, it was
a handerchief of sobs.

Obscene rose. Shared.
Loved.
Wounded mouth, nobody's breath.

Almost nothing.

Written shortly after the poet's travels to the U.S. in 1988, this book is certainly not de Andrade's strongest; but with a poem such as that above, one perceives why he is recognized as one of the most important poets of Portugal today.   —DM

*

Michael Palmer, Régis Bonvicino and Nelson Ascher, eds. *Nothing the Sun Could Not Explain: 20 Contemporary Brazilian Poets*. Los Angeles: Sun & Moon Press, 1997. 312 pages. $15.95

The first anthology of Brazilian poetry since Elizabeth Bishop's 1972 *An Anthology of Twentieth-Century Brazilian Poetry*, this major new work selects work from twenty poets writing post-concretist poetry in contemporary Brazil. The poets selected include important figures of the 1960s and 1970s, Paolo Leminski, Ana Cristina César, Torquato Neto, and Wally Salomão to younger figures of the 80s and 90s, Duda Machado, Horácio Costa, Angela De Campos, Claudia Roquette-Pinto, and the two Brazilian editors, Régis Bonvicino and Nelson Ascher.

* * *

Poetry in Spanish

Ernesto Livon Grosman, ed., *The XUL Reader: An Anthology of Argentine Poetry 1980-1996*, translated from the Spanish by Jorge Guitart, Kathryn A. Kopple, G. J. Racz, Graciela Sidoli, and Molly Weigel. New York: Roof Books, 1997. 136 pages. $15.95

The Argentine magazine XUL began publishing, with Jorge Santiago Perednik as editor, in the beginning of the 1980s, at the height of the mad military dictatorship that killed thousands of individuals. As editor Ernesto Livon Grosman writes, the poetry of its contributors was, in part, a reaction to the regime; but unlike the guerilla movements of the political left—with whom many contributors shared sympathies—the resistance took language itself as its method and subject. Like the American "Language" poets, the XUL writers sought in the purposeful complexity and density of words a way to resist the failed language of seemingly "transparent" statements of both sides, of both the victims and the victimizers—which as the editor points out, were interdependent for their existence. Like their American counterparts, these Argentine poets sought models in the avant-garde of the past, most particularly in the vernacularly-based poetry of the gaucho (or cowboy) poets, and in avant-gardists such as Oliverio Girondo, Xul Solar (one of the sources of the magazine's name), Osvaldo Lamborghini, and more recent authors such as Jorge Luis Borges and the Brazilian concretist, Augusto De Campos.

Writing in their fourth issue, a collective of XUL poets argued that their goal was to "translate." "To translate is to work in one language from another. Translating is the linguistic exercise that most privileges the breach between two texts because it is actually a previous reading that produces a new text in which writing claims to make a former text legible even as it disrupts and obfuscates one text by subtracting from it a legibility that it confers on another. …Translation only acquires significance, as far as XUL is concerned, when it affirms itself as a writing process that voluntarily exhibits its relation to other texts." A little further in this statement the XUL writers proclaim what might have as easily appeared in the pages of *L=A=N=G=U=A=G=E* magazine (edited by Bruce Andrews and Charles Bernstein): "XUL's committment to reality is actually a commitment to language: to again make legible that which has been used for coercion and deception. Language belongs to everyone."

This revelatory anthology begins with a few examples of the historical influences upon the XUL writers, themselves (particularly Giorondo and Xul Solar) worthy of further exploration, and then presents work selected from the ten issues of the journal. Each reader will find his or her own favorites, but given the context of the few pages devoted to each poet, I was most impressed by the work of Laura Klein, Néstor Perlongher, Susana Cerdá, Ernesto Livon Grosman, and the *XUL* editor Jorge Santiago Perednik. I was less taken with the concretist influenced work as evidenced in the poetry of Arturo Carrera, Gustavo Röessler, and Jorge Lépore — but that may just be my own aesthetic at work or a product of the anthologization. The important thing is that this is a truly brilliant collection of writing that cannot be ignored for anyone interested in contemporary, innovative poetry.

Although the poems are presented bi-lingually, I do wish the Spanish had appeared *enface* instead in small type at the bottom each page; and I am desparate for biographical material and source information for the poets included. But these are small quibbles with a book of such significance.   —*DM*

* * *

Poetry in Turkish

Ece Ayhan. *A Blind Cat Black* and *The Orthodoxies*, translated from the Turkish, with an Afterward by Murat Nemet-Nejat. Los Angeles: Sun & Moon Press, 1997. 96 pages. $10.95

Two collections of the great contemporary Turkish poet, Ece Ayhan, are translated in this small volume. As the translator writes in his afterword about the second of these volumes: "Ece Ayhan moved to the streets of Istanbul. The poem delves into the underbelly of the city, Galata, historically both its red light district — of transvestites, girl and boy prostitutes, tattooed roughs, heroin merchants, that is, the unnamed or 'euphemized' outcasts of Turkish culture — and the district where minorities — Armenians, Greeks, Jews, Russians, etc. — lived."

**POETRY FROM
SUN & MOON CLASSICS**

from the American
David Antin *Selected Poems: 1963–1973* $13.95
Djuna Barnes *The Book of Repulsive Women* $6.95
Charles Bernstein *Content's Dream: Essays 1975–1984* $14.95
Charles Bernstein *Dark City* 11.95
Charles Bernstein *Rough Trades* $10.95
Charles Bernstein *The Sophist* $11.95
David Bromige *The Harbormaster of Hong Kong* $10.95 [Canada]
Clark Coolidge *The Crystal Text* $11.95
Clark Coolidge *Own Face* $10.95
Clark Coolidge *The Rova Improvisations* $11.95
Ray DiPalma *Numbers and Tempers* $11.95
Barbara Guest *Defensive Rapture* $11.95
Barbara Guest *Fair Realism* $10.95
Lyn Hejinian *The Cell* $11.95
Lyn Hejinain *The Cold of Poetry* $12.95
Lyn Hejinian *My Life* $9.95
Lyn Hejinian *Writing Is an Aid to Memory* $9.95
Susan Howe *The Europe of Trusts: Selected Poems* $10.95
Jackson Mac Low *From Pearl Harbor Day to FDR's Birthday* $10.95
Jackson Mac Low *Pieces O' Six* $11.95
Carl Rakosi *Poems 1923–1941* $12.95
Jerome Rothenberg *Gematria* $11.95
Gilbert Sorrentino *The Orangery* $10.95
Gertrude Stein *Stanzas in Meditation* $11.95
Gertrude Stein *Tender Buttons* $9.95
John Taggart *Loop* $11.95
Barrett Watten *Frame (1971–1990)* $13.95
John Wieners *707 Scott Street* $12.95

from the British
Tom Raworth *Eternal Sections* $9.95

from the Dutch
Cees Nooteboom *The Captain of the Butterflies* $11.95

from the French
Pierre Alferi *Natural Gaits* $10.95
André du Bouchet *Where Heat Looms* $12.95
André Breton *Arcanum 17* $12.95
André Breton *Earthlight* $12.95
Henri Deluy *Carnal Love* $11.95
Dominique Fourcade *Click-Rose* $10.95
Dominique Fourcade *xbo* $9.95

from the German
Paul Celan *Breathturn* $12.95 [Bukovina/France]
Friederike Mayröcker *with each clouded peak* $11.95 [Austria]

from the Ancient Greek
Sappho *Poems* $10.95

from the Italian
Luigi Ballerini *The Cadence of a Neighboring Tribe* $10.95
Rosita Copioli *The Blazing Lights of the Sun* $11.95
Milo De Angelis *Finite Intuition* $11.95
Alfredo Giuliani, ed. *I Novissimi* $14.95
Antonio Porta *Metropolis* $10.95
Giuseppe Steiner *Drawn States of Mind* $8.95

from the Latin
Sextus Propertius *Charm* $10.95

from the Norwegian
Paal-Helge Haugen *Wintering with the Light* $10.95

from the Russian
Arkadii Dragomoschenko *Description* $11.95
Arkadii Dragomoschenko *Xenia* $12.95

from the Spanish
Susana Thénon *distancias/distances* $10.95 [Argentina]

from the Swedish
Claes Andersson *What Became Words* $11.95 [Finland]

from the Turkish
Ece Ayhan *A Blind Cat Black* and *Orthodoxies* $10.95

For a complete list of titles, write to
Sun & Moon Press, 6026 Wilshire Boulevard, Los Angeles, CA 90036

THE AMERICA AWARDS

(The "Ferns" Instituted in Memory of Anna Fahrni)

c/o The Contemporary Arts Educational Project, Inc. · 6026 Wilshire Boulevard · Los Angeles, California 90036
T (213) 857-1115   **F** (213) 857-0143   **E** djmess@sunmoon.com

Winners for 1997

INTERNATIONAL

Friederike Mayröcker

(Austria)
JUDGES: Peter Constantine, Peter Glassgold, Douglas Messerli
Marjorie Perloff, Paul Vangelisti, Mac Wellman

BELLES LETTRES AND SELECTED OR COLLECTED WORKS

Collected Works, Vols I–III, by Paul Metcalf

(Coffee House Press)
JUDGES: Joan Retallack, Jerome Rothenberg, Wendy Walker

DRAMA

Throwin' Bones, by Matthew Maguire

(La Mama/Creation Production Company, New York)
JUDGES: John Jesurun, Susan Mosakowski, Ronald Tavel

FICTION

Echoes, by Dennis Barone

(Potes and Poets)
JUDGES: Carla Harryman, Tom La Farge, Robert Steiner

POETRY

The Silhouette of the Bridge, by Keith Waldrop

(Avec Books)
JUDGES: Charles Bernstein, Norma Cole, Marjorie Welish

SERIES · 1997

I

Lyn Hejinian, *A Book From A Border Comedy*

Joe Ross, *The Wood Series*

Mohammed Dib, *Omneros*

Catriona Strang, *Steep: A Performance Notebook*

SERIES · 1998

2

Clark Coolidge, *Book of Stirs*

Giovanna Sandri, *Hourglass: The Rhythm of Traces*

Robert Crosson, *Bleeding Hearts, A Shallow Mercy*

Eléni Sikélianòs, *The Lover's Numbers*

Subscription: $25.00 per series · Series 1 (1997) titles
now available individually for $6.25 · Order from:
12011 Rochester Avenue Nº 9, Los Angeles, CA 90025.

RIBOT 6 — Over 60 Under 30

Presenting the work of poets and visual artists from around the world, born before 1938 or after 1968. Included are established figures such as John Baldessari, Amiri Baraka, Louise Bourgeoise, Henri Deluy, Mohammed Dib, Barbara Guest, Llyn Foulkes, Charles Garabedian, George Herms, Carlos Illescas, Friederike Mayröcker, Giulia Niccolai, Elio Pagliarani, Betty Saar, Nathaniel Tarn, Keith and Rosmarie Waldrop, as well as many young and emerging writers and artists.

In both editorial and graphic presentation, *Ribot* has established new standards as one of the most exciting literary and arts publications in the country. Featuring to date more than 200 writers and visual artists: Guy Bennett, Wallace Berman, Charles Bernstein, Karen Carson, Frank Chin, Michelle T. Clinton, Norma Cole, Corrado Costa, Robert Crosson, Enzo Cucchi, Giuliano Della Casa, Ray DiPalma, Jill Giegerich, Michael C. McMillen, Douglas Messerli, Margaret Nielsen, Dennis Phillips, Lari Pittman, Carl Rakosi, Martha Ronk, Jerome Rothenberg, Christina Peri Rossi, Giovanna Sandri, Leslie Scalapino, Aaron Shurin, Alexis Smith, Fernando Sorrentino, Gilbert Sorrentino, Adriano Spatola, Don Suggs, Diane Ward, Patty Wickman, Mac Wellman, Tom Wudl, William Xerra, Kevin Young and many others.

Paul Vangelisti, editor. John Clark & Looking LA, design.

Ribot 1 – Subversion (1993), *Ribot 2* – Public Service (1994), *Ribot 3* – Beauty (1995), *Ribot 4* –Fiction (1996) and *Ribot 5* – History (1997) are still available. The annual publication of the College of Neglected Science. All issues $9.95.

Ribot is distributed by Consortium Book Distribution and is part of **L.A. Books**, the cooperative of literary magazines and publishers based in Los Angeles. Visit us at **www.litpress.com**

LITTORAL BOOKS

NEW FROM LITTORAL BOOKS

George Albon, *Empire Life*, 72 pages, $10.95

The first, full-length edition of Albon's work is a much anticipated event. *Empire Life* brings together two long pieces: the title poem, 88 short 8-line lyrics, is a workaday fleshing out of time spent under inner and outer American weathers; while "Cosmophagy," marks a daring incursion into the heart of the sentence serving as both guide and treacherous ground.

Ray DiPalma, *Letters*, 72 pages, $10.95

Recently completed, many sections of this new and ambitious book-length work have been published over the last several years in journals throughout the U.S. and abroad. *Letters* is both public and private, exploiting the varied dynamics of correspondence, and a critical desire to renew and transcend the personal and historic past.

Previous tittles from Littoral still available: Amiri Baraka's *Funk Lore*, Norma Cole's *My Bird Book*, Fanny Howe's *The End*, Douglas Messerli's *Along Without* and *The Walls Come True*, Stephen Ratcliffe's *Sculpture*, Martha Ronk's & Don Sugg's *Desert Geometries*, Paul Vangelisti's *Villa* and Pasquale Verdicchio's *Isthmus*.

A centrally important new magazine.
— MARK PREJSNAR

Startling, exciting, one of the most spectacular magazine around. — ROBERT CROSSON

From the perspective of eternity, a truly multivalent collection of new writers in dialogue with proven writers forming an intensity-machine that tugs the mind in all directions at once, definitely worth coming back for.
— GILLES DELEUZE

Limited only by the fact that you have only two eyes, two ears, one lifetime. — FELIX GUATARI

RHIZOME is an annual journal of innovative poetry, visual arts, and reviews. ¶ Former Issues have included: Barbara Guest, Tan Lin, Paul Vangelisti, Dennis Phillips, Ray DiPalma, Norma Cole, Cole Swensen, Leslie Scalapino, Mark Wallace, Juliana Spahr, Jacques Debrot, George Albon, Guy Bennett, Martha Ronk, Nick Piombino, John Lowther, Nico Vassilakis, Brian Strang, Noemi Maxwell, Aaron Shurin, Michael Gottlieb, Robert Crosson, John Yau, Mac Wellman, Douglas Messerli, Amiri Baraka, Pierre Alferi, Catriona Strang, John Taggart, Bruce Andrews, Charles Bernstein, Martine Bellen, Spencer Selby, Michael Gizzi, Stephen Ratcliffe, Joe Ross, Steve Carll, Sheila Murphy, Paul Long, Graham Foust, Andrew Mossin, Franklin Bruno and many others.

Send check for $10 to Standard Schaefer
366 South Mentor Avenue #108
Pasadena, CA 91106